an

ANIMAL ANTICS

—*2004*—

Vol III

Edited by
Sarah Marshall

First published in Great Britain in 2004 by Anchor Books
Remus House, Coltsfoot Drive, Peterborough, PE2 9JX
Tel (01733) 898102
SB ISBN 1-84418-289-4

Foreword

Anchor Books is a small press, established in 1992, with the aim of promoting readable poetry to as wide an audience as possible.

We hope to establish an outlet for writers of poetry who may have struggled to see their work in print.

The poems presented here have been selected from many entries, and as always editing proved to be a difficult task.

I trust this selection will delight and please the authors and all those who enjoy reading poetry.

Sarah Marshall
Editor

Contents

To Dino

My cat is fantastic, all furry and fun.
Loves to sit by the fire or bask in the sun.
I'm forced to take notice - though TV's my intention,
Cos your soft gentle paws, pad my arm for attention,
Then you'll sit nice and warm, relaxed on my knees,
Knowing well that I like it, you just aim to please.
You're purring away quite happy in sleep,
Until you decide that it's time for a leap!
So off you streak, stand and stretch every bit
Of your body and limbs, with wide yawning lip.
You look up at me then with questioning eyes,
'Is it time for a feed?' your soft miaow cries.
And when I call 'Dino', you come on all fours
As we both greet each other - you are mine - and I'm yours.

A Cotter

The Golden Girls

Sun streaks through the trees
and passes her by
yawning and stretching
she opens her eyes.

With patience and purpose
she struggles to wake
moving silently forward
to open the gate.

She greets her companion
and falls into line
moving in sequence
stopping to dine.

They circle the garden
then resting awhile
They cuddle together
making me smile.

Who would have thought it?
The best of friends
Curious playmates
a dog and a hen!

Sandra Evans

Hattie's Song

Sleek creature
Shiny smooth
Unsure at times
She needs reassurance
Love
Touching
Verbal tunes

She jumps up onto my knee
Singing Hattie's song
It comes from deep in her throat
She settles down to soft purrs

We call it 'Hattie's song'.

Moira Jean Clelland

Fish

My tank full of fish,
They would make a nice dish,
If you didn't want them
as pets,
But I look after them so they need no vets.

My tank full of fish,
Every day I make a wish,
A fish I hope to be,
So that they can play with me.

My tank full of fish,
When they go I will miss
Watching their mouths open and close,
And to the others they seem to pose!

Catrina Lawrence

Our Dog Slikker

In all the world there is no dog
Like our dog, Slikker,
There is no canine, half so fine,
As our dog, Slikker,
You should see him jump and wag his tail,
When he runs outside to get the mail
Our clever dog, Slikker.

He lies on the mat and pretends he's asleep,
Does our dog, Slikker,
But through his lashes, he will peep,
Will our dog, Slikker.
He'll jump up high and rush about,
If he thinks I'm going to take him out
Will our dog, Slikker.

He loves to play a merry game,
Does our dog, Slikker,
With balls or bones, they're all the same,
To our dog, Slikker.
He'll growl and bark, and leap and bound
And toss the balls and bones around
Will our dog, Slikker.

I hope he's with us for many a day
Our dear dog, Slikker.
For no other dog could with us play,
Like our dog, Slikker.
He likes to climb upon my knee,
No dog could mean the same to me
As our belovèd Slikker.

Rosanna J Freeman

14

My Frisbee

Running left then running right
I watch it duck and dive
It swirls around then lifts again
And I am left behind.

Up in the air it catches the breeze
And dances out of reach,
With one big effort I leap full height
And catch it in my teeth!

Cyd Griffin

The Ice Cream Cone

A lovely summer's day,
in the beautiful county of Cornwall
was the perfect setting, and a bench
with an ice cream cone in my hand
was the perfect thing to do

So to the window of the shop,
I asked the lady with a smiling face
for a 'Vanilla flavour please,'
anxiously looking at a nearly empty tub.

Not to worry, there was plenty for one
'and a little cone for your little dog'
who was looking so expectantly
and she received it with pleasure!

My dear little Pomeranian
knew she had been give a lovely
treasure and enjoyed it to the full,
it was the one and only one
she ever had and it was her last.

I still can smile when I dream
of my little dog and often wonder if
that kind lady ever realised the joy
she had given to both of us on a
sunny afternoon in Bude.

J L Holden

Glen

How could anyone abandon you?
I really don't know, I haven't a clue,
Small and sweet, a living soul,
Not left with anything, not even a bowl.

All over town you walked and ran,
Your little body, black, white and tan,
No food or water, looking for a bite,
This is just cruel, it isn't right.

A Jack Russell just looking for care,
You must have gone just anywhere,
Up the road, down the street,
All you wanted was someone kind to meet.

Then someone came and took you away,
You were just a little stray,
They took you, cared for you, treated you well,
Took you away from that living hell!

We heard about you waiting for a home,
How hard it was when you had to roam,
We saw you with your loving eyes,
Those horrible people we truly despise.

Now you are ours, our darling Glen,
You will never go through that ever again,
You are so special in our heart,
With us forever, we will never be apart.

Pearl Devereux

Sad Times

It's funny how my mind went blank, when in his eyes I stared
And only later did I think, on all the times we'd shared
They said he didn't have much time, the tumour's gotten worse
I heard words like 'inoperable' . . . now I'm waiting on the worst.

I remember when he was so young, the day we brought him home
How everyone did make a fuss, all the 'oohs' and 'aahs' intoned
We'd put him in his bed at night and before you closed the door
He'd be dreaming in the 'land of nod' to the tune of a gentle snore

I recalled a summer's garden, when we'd chased a rolling ball
With his little legs and no control, how he'd tumble and he'd fall
With eyes so brown and clear, with sandy hair but short
Made easy friends with everyone, for he was a gentle sort

Who always had a sense of fun, yet I'd never seen him fear
I'd turn around and there he was . . . like magic just appear
He was both true and faithful, and he learned his lessons well
And though he was no Einstein, he was clever you could tell

I thought upon such times we'd shared, times both laughed and cried
And then it was he closed his eyes, just slipped away . . . and died!
My wife and children shed their tears, but I refused to grieve
For the blessing that had been his life and the memories he did leave

We'll miss him and his friendship, those memories will not dim
Of big brown eyes and sorry looks, though gone . . . we still sense him
Only now the times remembered . . . with happiness and joy
Midst the echo of a barking dog and cries of 'Come on, boy'

I believe God waits in paradise, makes a place for me and you
And as He was a carpenter, then maybe . . . maybe kennels too
For the sixteen years we'd loved him, he'd earned this and his keep
It's funny how my mind went blank . . . when they put my dog to sleep!

M J Banasko

Walkies!

'Come on, Lady. Get your lead'
My mistress says to me.
If I pretend I haven't heard,
Perhaps she'll let me be
She thinks I need the exercise,
But really! Can't she see
Tucked up on these cushions,
Is where I'd rather be?
I think the one who wants the walk
Isn't me but she!
So she should go and get the lead
And take herself, not me!

Margaret Doherty

Rosie

When Rosie came to our house
She really was quite small
Silvery grey and fluffy
Around her eyes a curl.

Rosie is now growing up
She really is a size
White and grey and curly
Soulful liquid eyes

The tiny yap now has gone
Instead, a deep, deep bark
Yet Rosie is a softie
She's only having a laugh

She bounds around the garden
On her enormous feet
Chasing bees and butterflies
And once it was a leaf

Rosie is our sheepdog
I'm sure you must have guessed
Our gentle loving giant
Rosie really is the best!

Juliet Marshall

Dillon's Dilemma

Oh there's that perishing lead again
I suppose it's time for my walk
I'd much rather stay in my basket
If only I could talk
It's not that I don't like the walkies
It's the tugging that makes me fed up
And all those grown up people
Telling her she must train her pup
After all I cannot help sniffing
All those wonderful smells out there
To expect me to patter straight past them
Is really just so unfair
There, she's calling me, I had better go
And let her get me ready
I don't suppose we will get too far
Before she is saying, 'Steady!'

Susan Anthony

My Dog

He's not tall, but small
But he's proud and stands up tall,
He's a cinnamon shade of red,
And is very fluffy on his head,
Yes, you've guessed, he is a chow,
And every time I walked past someone, they say, 'Wow!'

His eyes are as black as night,
And his tail is snow-white,
His feet are like a bear's,
And he drags them along like he doesn't care!

When he's on a leash, he's like a bull,
And you heave him back with a great big pull!

He is very obedient,
He knows, 'roll over, 'paw' and 'sit',
And I won't stop loving him,
Till I get to the bottom of the bottomless pit!

Jessica Copland

Charlie's Angel

'Who's that knocking at my door?'
'Who's that walking down my street?'
'Don't come near, I'm not the kind of dog you would like to meet.'

All I wanted was a faithful pet
A Labrador - that's what I'll get!
A bundle of joy, just seven weeks old
The light of our lives, a dog to behold.
A little yellow Labrador, Charlie was his name,
To him life was fun, all just a game.

Charlie had so much energy, he would surely calm down soon
But his favourite was the 'wall of death' around the sitting room
'Stop that Charlie, no, don't do that,
What was that scream? Oh no, he is mounting the cat!'

He was fast and strong with teeth you couldn't ignore
- Not your usual Labrador.

Walk after walk, but still he wanted more
- No, not your usual Labrador.

And as the months passed by, it wasn't much fun
Charlie was different, something had to be done.

First stop the vet, 'Is medication what we require?'
'Castration is the answer, it's because he's entire!'
He was duly castrated - cat-safe at last
'But, what about his problems?' 'Well I'm glad that you asked!

You need a behaviourist, an expert in his field,
A consultation, a training plan, yes, that's what you need!'

Two experts later, and armed with a list of his needs:
A head collar, a harness, a collection of leads
A bumbag and titbits and mandatory clicker.
'Keep up with the training, this way will be quicker!'
So strapped up in his harness, bumbag at the ready
Someone coming towards us, trying to keep him steady.

But as they approached, it was all in vain
Teeth gnashing and snarling - it was always the same;
Lunging and barking, 'I'm not going to be beat;
No - I'm not the kind of dog you would like to meet!'

What was I do? Should I do the deed?
He's the love of my life, but way out of my league.
Then a ray of light shone, was it divine intervention?
I was reading the paper and Rod Roberts was mentioned.

A dog training course was advertised, and after it Rod's name
'Help for all types of problem dogs'. Rod knew the game.
'All the things about Charlie's behaviour you hate,
Well they're his greatest assets; no it's not too late.'

Rod duly took us both under his wing
Guiding us, training us, through thick and thin.
'Working Trials is what we are working toward,
Charlie needs stimulation and a purpose to stop him getting bored.'

Surely enough Charlie's confidence grew
And even became friendly with people he knew.
He began to enjoy life, 'People weren't that bad,
They fussed me and stroked me and what about that sausage I had?'

Now he is competing in Working Trials and it's all down to Rod
He has given Charlie his life back; he is such a happy dog.

'Who's that knocking at my door?
Who's that walking down my street?
I am Charlie! Just the kind of dog you would like to greet!'

Janet Freeman

My Tiny Tiger

He has a tiger's elegance
But on a smaller scale,
A rounded form with darker rings
Like bracelets on his tail.

His coat is just as smooth and svelte
But of a smaller size.
He has the same designer stripes,
The same gold-glitter eyes.

He paces as a tiger does,
Making a tiny swathe
Through crystal grass where silver mice
In pools of moonlight bathe.

He stops, he lies in wait and then
On priceless fields he crouches,
Bejewelled by the sapphire bells
That make exotic couches.

He has a tiger's lordly stance,
His bold, hypnotic stare,
His grace of movement when he walks,
His proud, imperious air.

He has the same intelligence,
The same instinctive skill,
And tiger-like he walks alone
And has a tiger's will.

If fate should compromise my cat
So these two creatures met,
He'd fire on all compressors
To take off like a jet.

Celia G Thomas

Ode To Puss Catt

I welcome the day
My friend came to stay
And for the gifts
He so freely gives.
At first just a shadow,
A glimpse in the dark
And a bowl
Which was licked, oh, so clean.

Now he is sleek
And happy with life.
His presence
He openly shows.
Each mouse in the house
Ev'ry rat in the barn,
Shook at the sound of his name.

Dear Puss Catt
Old friend cat
You're worth every Kit-E-Kat,
Tho' foe of poor Pansy the dog.
Your agile nobility
And friendly notoriety,
You're the king
Of this rodent-free home!

Lyn Sandford

My Furry Friend

I have a furry friend who is cute and cuddly.
Tiger is his name, a name he lives up to.
Always swinging on the curtains, scaring the living
daylights out of the budgie.
I know he would like to eat the goldfish as a treat.
Always near beside me, he is lying now at my feet.
Purring, singing and swatting flies.
Ah sure, he is always full of mischief, my little pride and joy.
I could not be without him.
My tiger!

Nancy Elliott

My Cat Tigger

Tigger was my wonder cat, with such a common name
He really was exclusive; he could drive me quite insane
His colour was all ginger, apart from his pink nose
And his hair was always falling out; covered all my clothes,

Whenever we moved house, which was often in the past
He had to re-establish himself with every other cat!
His territory he would claim; ferocious he did fight
Battle-scarred he'd come home, a weary cat that night

We always had a cat door, so he could wander in and out
Once he brought a black tail in, from another cat no doubt
He seemed to climb the highest, of any cat around
Rescued from a building, sometimes he hit the ground!

Yet he was very loveable, he'd sit on anyone's knee
Never showed a preference, could be a he or she!
Sadly showed his signs of age when he reached nineteen
We had to take him to a vet; you all know what I mean.

He was buried in the garden, beneath a lovely rose
The sweetest cat in my world, now sleeping in repose
Such a strong affection, I developed for my cat
I'd love to see him once again, just sitting on my lap.

Joan Prentice

My Faithful Friend, Simba

My dog is my best friend, he is with me all the time,
No finer pal in all the world I could ever find.
He is so loyal and trusting, he never lets me down,
And when I feel lonely he is always around.
His big brown eyes look up to me and a kind word I do say,
Then he comes and licks my hand, what more can I say?

Don Goodwin

My Sunshine Budgie

Once I had a budgie called Becky.
A bright yellow colour she was,
      and what a pretty sight she made.
She was also a chirpy little thing.
Strong and long-lived, she outlived
      three other budgies of mine.
Tame she was not, a solitary,
      strong budgie, my Becky.
When I went to touch her,
      she would bite and struggle free.
Left alone she wanted to be,
      just to look pretty and majestic.
Her alones made her strong.
But one day she started struggling
      with her flying.
It didn't get any better,
      so to the vet I took her.
The vet couldn't find anything wrong.
'Just old age,' said he,
      'nobody lives forever.'
One day, soon after, I found her dead
      at the bottom of her cage.
At the end of her life
      she'd been struggling and suffering.
For seven and a half years she lived,
      during which she taught me something;
'You can make it on your own. Be strong.'
At rest she is now and may God keep her.

Christina Gilbert

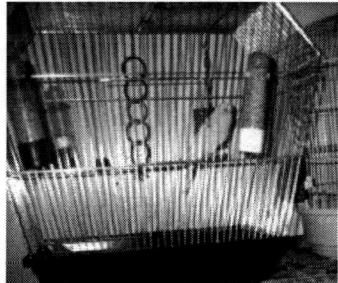

A Faithful Dog

A dog is a man's best friend,
you can teach him tricks
make him run for sticks
and give him treats, no end.
He's playful and fun
and loves to run,
you walk for miles and miles,
he jumps through hoops
and runs through fields
and leaps over crooked stiles.
At times of rest
near the fireplace is best,
as it's cosy and warm you know,
he's your very best friend
and true to the end
when you're down
and feeling low.
When times are good
when times are bad,
a dog is your favourite mate,
when you finish work
and arrive home late,
he's there waiting
for you at the gate.

Rachael Ford

Cat's Life!

'Dusty! Dusty!' Did I hear my mistress call?
Oops! I'm all tangled up in her 'wool' ball,
I'm in trouble again, will she scold me?
No . . . she laughs out loud as she sets me free,
I tried to make friends with the bird in the cage,
But it nipped my nose and flew into a rage,
When I dipped my paw in the goldfish bowl,
The cold water startled me, on the floor it did roll,
I didn't like getting wet, I did soon discover,
So escaping into the garden, I ran for cover,
With all this excitement, I needed a 'wee',
I wonder how far I can climb up that tree,
I've got to the top, it's scary looking down,
As I cling on and cry, I see a face with a frown,
Soon two loving arms gently enfold me,
And take me safely indoors in time for tea.

Glenice Siddall

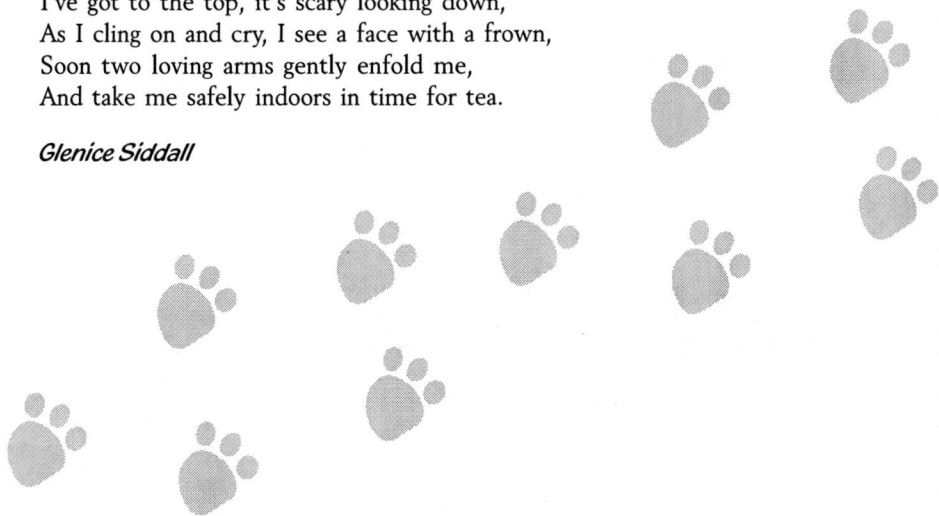

The Badger Gasps and Groans

When midnight comes a host of dogs and men come out to play.
Go out and track the badger to his den,
And put a sack within his hole and lie there -
Till the old grunting badger passes by.
He comes and hears - they let the strongest loose.
The old fox hears the noise and drops the goose.
The poacher shoots and hurries from the cry,
And the old hare, wounded, buzzes by.
They get a forked stick to bear him down -
And clap the dogs and take him into town
And bait him all the day with many dogs
And laugh and shout and fight the scampering hogs.
He runs along and bites at all he meets:
The shout and holler down the noisy streets.

He turns to about to face the loud uproar . . .
And drives the rebels to their very door.
The frequent stone is hurled where'er they go;
Your disposition so sweet, no one else could ever compete.
You were dignified and classy right from the start.
Love was what you were about; of this, there's no doubt.
You are my 'brown dogs' for keeps.
When badgers fight, then everyone's a foe!

The dogs are clapped and urged to join the fray;
The badger turns and drives them all away.
Through it, though scarcely half as big, demure and small -
He fights with dogs for hours and beats them all.
The heavy mastiff, savage in the fray,
Lies down and, like it, licks his feet and turns away.
The bulldog knows his match and waxes cold,
The badger grins and never leaves his hold.
He drives the crowd and follows at their heels -
And lets them through - the drunkard swears and reels.

The frightened women take the boys away,
The blackguard laughs and hurries on the fray,
Till kicked and torn and beaten, out he lies -
And leaves his hold and cackles, groans and dies!

Viv Lionel Borer

Fluffy

Fluffy was a flighty mouse
Made of mighty stuff
Quiet in his whitey house
Most content enough

Out about on mousy walk
On tippy, tappy toe
Housey mousey, 'round the housey
Mousily would go

Scatty, scutter, skittering
Scatters 'round the room
Scatty catty comes to chase . . .
Fluffy with a zoom

Flighty to his whitey house
Fluffy nears the door
Yet! Too late for fluffy fluff
Fluff all 'round the floor.

Gemini Cherry

Mixed-Up Pets

I called my terrier, Kitty, my cat I named Rover.
These names confused them, a problem they could not get over.

So Rover took over if a stray cat should stray.
She did all the doggy things and chased it away.

Now terrier Kitty what a pity did something new.
Drank milk from a saucer and started to mew.

With this unfair confusion I reversed the illusion changing back their
        names although they
Could not accept the fact that they had been changed around the other way.

The terrier is now living at a cats' home and Kitty herds sheep in north Wales.
Or is this another one of those 'shaggy dog tales'?

T A Napper

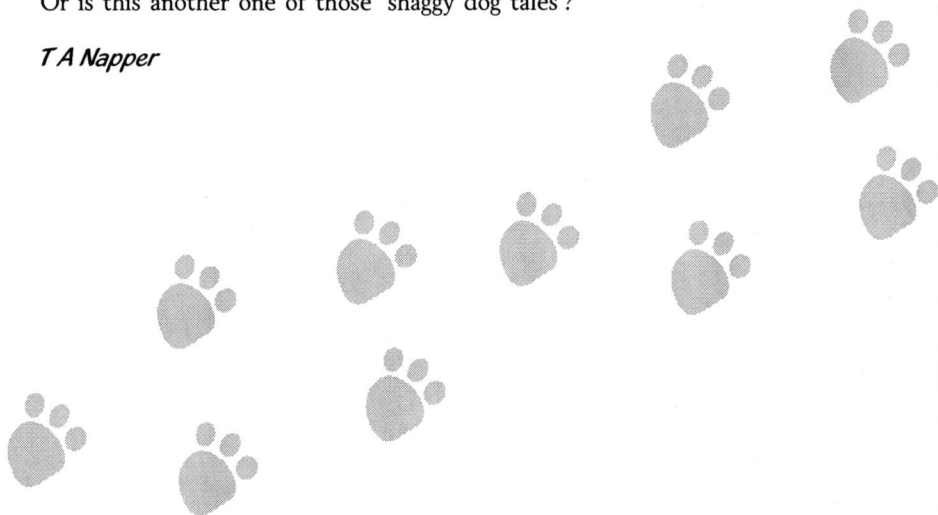

My Cat

I've had my cat since he was born
I've watched him grow, I've watched him yawn
Scratch the furniture, make a mess
But I still love my cat the best

He loves to drink milk, eat tuna too
He sits on your lap and purrs for you
You let him out, he comes back in
You play games, he lets you win

I brush his fur coat every day
He listens to what I have to say
If cats could talk what tales they'd tell
About all other cats and dogs as well

I'd never part with my dear cat
The way he sits on the mat
The way he comes when you call
I love my cat best of all.

Sally Anne Petrie

Compromised Freedom

Little brown feathery bird
Up in your 'wherry' nest
Singing happily, free as a bird
Well, really, so you should be

Early in the crow of dawn
Off you go in search of worms.
How diligent you are in your chores;
Make way, Make way! And here you come.

I watch with envy and excitement
As you dole out with love and commitment.
What a way to live a life,
Full of misery and imprisonment.

A pet I took for you to be,
But your freedom it compromised.
I promise with my heart to let you go
Once your chicks are strong,
And ready to fly.

Emmanuel Omoro

A Kitten's Plea

'Miaow!' She lets out a pitiful cry.
She has not yet seen the land or sky.
Her eyes are closed to the world around her.
All she can hear is her sibling's purr.

They grow silent, she is left all alone
As they cry out their final moan.
This tabby kitten dumped in a cardboard box.
Left to the mercy of any dog or fox.

'Miaow!' Will someone not hear her plea?
'Miaow! Can someone please find me?'
Dumped by an adult in a wheelie bin.
Don't they know it's a crime and a sin?

Helpless she is not completely alone.
All she wants is that perfect home.
A comfy lap to curl up on at night.
If someone knew of her plight.

Curled up in front of a log fire.
Is only this kitten's one desire!
Cute and cuddly she deserves a home.
Not to be left in a box all on her own.

How can people be so cruel?
Can we not make a tighter rule?
No animals should start his or her life this way.
People who commit cruelty should be put away.

Jo Lodge

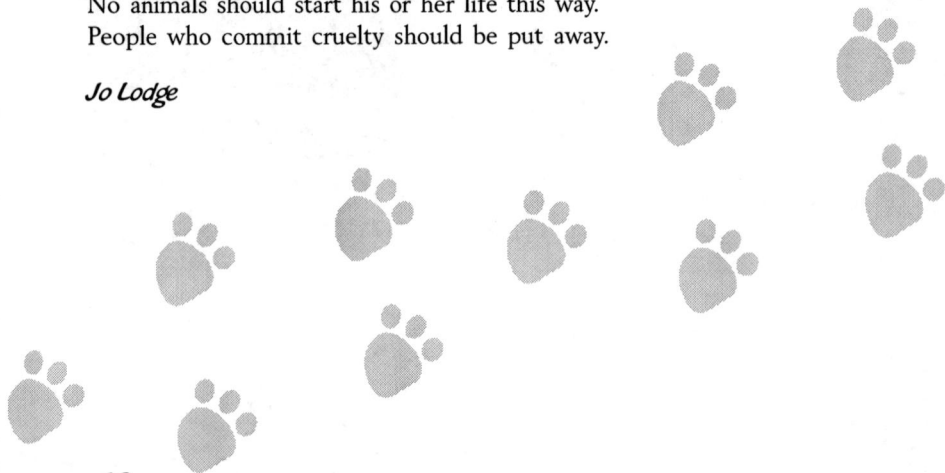

Of Mice And Milk

When cats curl and yawn
To snooze and sleep,
What dreams may come
To tickle feet?

When whiskers twitch
Do they pursue
That squeak of mouse
Yet out of view?

When tails do flick
So swift and fast,
Are they pouncing through
The dewy grass?

Or when snoozing there
As soft as silk,
Do they dream of saucers
Charg'd with milk?

M Sam Dixon

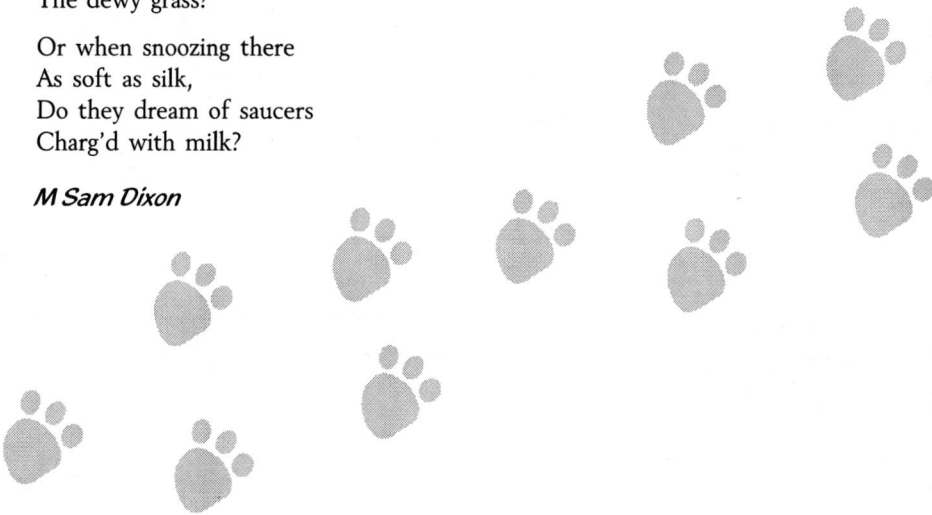

Ben

I'm glad you chose me to be the one
For you give me strength to carry on
You are my friend when I'm feeling low
My pal when I've nowhere to go
You listen without making a sound
And are there when I need someone around

You look at me with love in your eyes
There's no way in your look, could your eyes ever lie.
My brave heart, that's what you are to me
My Ben, my dog, my friend you will always be.

Maureen Morris

Blue!

Five years ago to the day
I received what I had been wishing for.
A man got a message from the SPCA
A girl wanted a husky that he had to give away

He came to my house with a tear in his eye
He said, 'This is Blue and he is very shy.'
It took a while, but the shyness melted away
Our family grew and loved each day

Long walks we would take
And he loved car rides to the lake
He wanted to spend his time outside
But, also loved rough housing inside

Time is shorter than you think
It can be gone quicker than a blink
My dream growing up was to have Blue
It is now just a memory of a dream come true

Out of my touch
It hurts so much
A life now lost, had so much to give
Now, I am lost and have to live!

Paula Brewer

Billy, Our Clever Cultural Cat

He often takes in 'Mastermind'
Or other quizzes of that kind,
British Fashion Week is his forte;
Our Billy's *so* not 'prêt-a-porter'.
Models treading the catwalk -
Oh, if only our sweet Billy could talk!
He'd tell you everything that's new;
For now, he comments in purr and mew.

Billy, our clever cultural cat,
Adores the Proms, and events like that,
Men dressed, like him, in black and white
Playing instruments till late at night.
'Newsnight' and interviews by Paxman -
Not for him Superman and Batman.
His taste extends to opera and ballet,
Not 'Friends', or 'Cheers' with Kirstie Alley!

Billy, our clever cultural cat,
Transfixed by 'Time Team' and all that
As he digests the evening news
So trans*mog*rified become his views.
Following Palin on his travels,
Or, as life beneath the sea unravels,
Nature programmes seem to be the best,
For it's after these his eyes shut to rest.

Geraldine Laker

Puppy Love

When we saw Lucy she was a ball of fluff
Her damp cold nose and her small tongue was rough
When we gave her milk it was her favourite drink
Her noisy lapping was like tap water running at the sink

The name was chosen, it was Lucy for this beautiful one
The days we had with her became such contented fun
Those special treats, the petting she got when she was small
Those torn pieces of newspapers and toilet roll littered the hall

Those chewed slippers were always found in her small basket bed
When we scolded her, she would sulk and drop her forlorn head
We would always find her favourite toys upon an armchair
The cushions and carpet were covered with her fine strands of hair

She would always be a friend, this faithful, beautiful, loving pet
We would laugh when she struggled to climb those garden steps
The grass would be in a mess with her playthings and chewed bones
Thro' that large hole in the hedge she often crawled and roamed.

Thro' these special times our dog Lucy will always be our best friend
She grew so fast that sweet puppy love we hope will never end
These most cherished years here filled pleasures we love to share
Without our Lucy our lives and our hearts would be empty sitting there.

J Grainger

Puppy Love

She jumps up to lick my face
And excitement makes her wee!
When I come home to our place
She jumps up to lick my face!
My pup feels no disgrace
When she runs to welcome me,
She jumps up to lick my face,
And excitement makes her wee!

Dan Pugh

Eee Me Dog!

Eee, I love me dog
I love him more than any mog
He doesn't bite, he doesn't scratch
He doesn't wee on a certain patch

Eee, I love me pet
There's not another I'd rather get
He's very loyal, he's very tame
He gets his ball to play a game

Eee, I love me Scooby-Doo
When I chose him who knew
That he would be my best friend
Any troubles he would mend

Eee, I love me dog
If you're getting a pet don't get a frog
They're very cold with slimy skin
And how funny you'd look walking him!

Beverley Dale

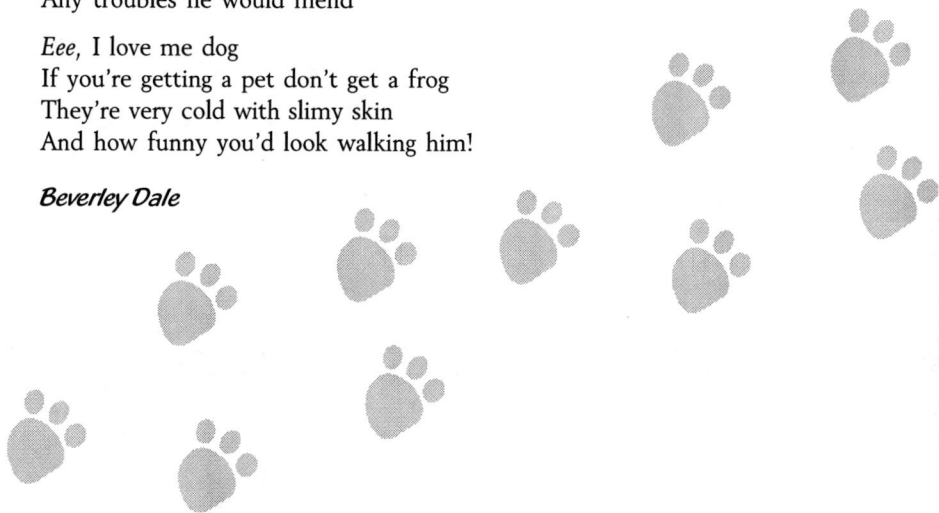

We Are Drawn!

Without the need of any spoken words - we are
all drawn by the antics of our pussy cat -

Will look at us with wide-open eyes - telling us
she is now ready for her treat - once given she
will purr until she falls asleep.

Over the years a trust has been built up - she knows
no harm will come from us - and she knows we
need a pussy cat - Lucy is her name!

R P Scannell

Animals Section - Mice In A Stew

Dearest eldest grandson, Josef

On my travels again
discovered and cross my heart and hope to die
this is true and they say there is proof

there is a place called Guang Zhou
which is said totally differently to the way it is spelt
but research keeps interfering with my sound system
so I find it difficult to familiarise myself with the language

this place is called Gwang Joe
which is in the vicinity of H Kong
the city, not Hitler's favourite film,
has mice which are five kilograms in weight
like a little pig, says my favourite Li Feng
these are mice not unlike the regular invaders from the sewers
of my London cottage where you used to visit
down round the corner of Idi Amin's wife's restaurant
who was done for a mucky kitchen by the council!

Josef, Guang Zhou mice are eaten alive for lunch
and scream but thrice . . .
they swore to me at Haier last night at lesson time
and swore this was so, and who am I to disbelieve Haier staff?

The first time when dipped into salt
the second time when bitten into
and the third time, I forget . . .
as I wasn't listening anymore, being a vegetarian
no, I've got it . . .
first when sliced, second when salted and third when bitten

and Josef, all Chinese people everywhere say
in Guang Zhou, they eat everything on benches
except the benches . . . !

Renate Fekete

A Puppy Called Basil

I rescued a puppy called Basil
He looked all forlorn and thin
My heart ruled my head when I saw him
So I took the poor blighter in.

I gave him my old Whitney blanket
Tried settling down by the hearth
But I could tell Basil was thinking
Yeah mate, you're having a laugh.

He yelped till three in the morning
The noise went right through my head
There was only one thing for it
I took Basil into my bed.

It put an end to his whining
And he slept for and hour or two
Then I woke to his licks and his barking
And a duvet all covered in poo.

It's six o'clock in the morning
My duvet's been thrown in the bin
We're sharing my old Whitney blanket
But I'm not sharing Basil's wry grin.

Now don't get me wrong, I adore him
It really was love at first sight
But I'm gonna sleep by the fire
And Basil can have my room tonight.

Trudy Simpson

Biggles

O' Biggles, tell me what it was,
That made you such a treasure,
Perhaps a multitude of traits,
Gave each of us such pleasure.

Maybe it was the 'tilted' head,
That seemed to check our mood!
Were *boots* or *opener* in mind?
Was it a walk or food?

Before a walk, you'd slip out quick,
And clear up Harry's plate,
Then, stopping by to grab your stick,
(Eyes firmly on the gate).

Across the common you would run,
With Harry chasing rabbits.
You'd yelp and bark and dodge and turn,
Endearing 'Biggy' habits.

If any one of us was sad,
You seemed to gauge our mood,
You'd 'flump' right down and snuggle in,
As if you understood.

You sensed your time clock running out,
So you knew what to do,
You gave us Algy, Bobbie, too,
A perfect gift from you.

So Biggy, as we've shared your life,
With walks, treats, bits of fuss,
A true companion, special friend.
Ben's dog, yet loved by us.

Gillian Humphries

Master Of His Realm

Do you own a cat? Does he do tricks?
Get into mischief, amuse with antics?
Mine does! Pooch! Colouring aping small tiger,
Intelligent feline, no other cat finer,
Lithe, handsome and striking, bounding swiftly along,
Muscular as a panther, for his size and age, strong,
Hunts prey, not to eat but paw - plonk on head,
He wants them to play, not rigid and dead.

In summer months never fails to wake me at dawn,
My head held with paw, combs mane with southpaw! I yawn and yawn!
He cat-preens me, claws out, sprucing hair down with tongue
When strands caught midst wee teeth, becomes highly-strung!
I let out piercing shriek, 'Stop! Tangled underneath!'
Pull out hair and ignore him but he's staring beneath,
Those amber eyes do not blink, directly bore into mine,
With smouldering glare, suddenly makes a beeline
To climb up my body till our noses entwine.

How can I resist a cat with such charm?
I know hour is early but he's doing no harm,
Pooch, gently nips my arm awaiting to be fed
From dry cat food packet kept beside bed,
Sated, he twists into air, returns to lie sleepy head
In cat bed; leaving me smiling at determined redhead.

Hilary Jill Robson

Old Dogs, Young Dogs

He's old, my old Ben
And I don't know just when
He could run as fast as the wind
Whereas my young Dibble
Runs like the debble
With the hop and the skip of a rebel

He's grouchy, my old Ben
And I don't know just when
He turned into a grumpy old fart
But Jack Russell Dibble
Is just dibble tribble
With more life than an engine's kick-start

He's a springer, old Ben
And I don't know just when
He first breathed on me 'breath of cod'
Or first angrily barked, in Dibble's face:
'Disgrace, disgrace, to the canine race
For letting them brush your teeth, bathe your face!'

He's old my old Ben
And I don't know just when
I loved him like I do now
But I love 'Jack the ripper'
The new town boy nipper
Old dogs, young dogs, all dogs are chipper!

Eric Ferris

Angel

A precious gift at Christmas time
The sweetest thing to see
Sleeping in a cardboard box
Beneath the festive tree

We named her 'Little Angel'
She only slept and purred
We thought that she was *purrrr-fect*
Until she killed a bird

Come spring we thought to decorate
New wallpaper we chose
But oh, one day, when we came home
She'd ripped it with her claws

From then we couldn't stop her
She went from bad to worse
Where was our little Angel
The pet we used to nurse?

And then one night dear Grandma
Lay resting in her bed
When she gave out the loudest scream
That you have ever heard!

'Come quickly, please come quickly
Something's nibbling at my feet'
We pulled away the blankets
A mouse was in the sheet

To think we'd called her Angel
So very funny that
She's no *little angel*
She's a very naughty *cat!*

Ann Donovan

Untitled

You may think that I am Santa Claus,
The hat gives me away,
I'm laid down in my armchair,
It's been a very busy day.

I ran the hedgerows, sniffed and played
Then my mistress called me back.
The days are getting shorter now,
And the skies are looking black.

My bed is this big armchair,
It's cosy, soft and warm.
My family call it *my* chair,
And I'll never come to harm,

This hat is just a joke you know,
I'm such a silly girl,
My mistress dressed me up like this,
But I'm too tired to do a twirl,

She put this on her Christmas cards,
I thought it was quite silly,
By the way, I'm not really Santa Claus,
My proper name is Tilly.

D Cordell

Ode To A Corgi

'What's that?' they say when I am out
'What *is* that on the lead?'
More Welsh than leeks and daffodils
Dwarf dog, this ancient breed.

The old-time farmers know that I'm
A herder not a hound,
Some say my legs are much too short,
But all four reach the ground!

'Is that a sausage with a tail?'
They say when they come round.
No, I'm a Cardigan corgi
Not a short sheepdog from the pound.

Paula Stevens

Is That Your Dog?

Dogs are a man's best friend,
They are faithful to the end,
There are no dogs the same,
There are no dogs just plain,
Because they have a personality of their own.

They may bark when the postman sings,
Or perhaps when the doorbell rings,
It really is a joy,
To see your dog play with its favourite toy,
Is your dog considerate and kind
And keeps thinking of you in heart and mind?

My dog, so happy, full of life,
Ready each day and gives no strife,
Nothing is too much for his dear heart,
My dog and I will never part.

Yes, that's my dog!

Amber Stevens

The Sweetest Pudding Of All

I didn't really want a dog, the two we had grew old,
We loved them both so very much, were worth their weight in gold.

My youngest son and daughter said, 'Please just can you see?'
I knew who would look after it, yes, that's right, just me.

We saw this advert mention, of puppies that were for sale,
When I knew the cost they were, my face just went quite pale.

A little Yorkshire terrier, aged two weeks to the day,
I rang the breeder there at once, 'Can we see her straightaway?'

The lady entered in the room, her palm stretched out and steady,
She said, 'This is the little dog, although she's not quite ready.'

Those piercing, shiny, sweetest eyes, were staring back at me,
I fell in love that moment, 'Can I take her home with me?'

We named her Little Pudding, as Yorkshire went with that,
Her fur coat coloured steel and tan, on your knee she often sat.

We watched her playful puppy ways, we took her everywhere,
Whenever you were feeling down, Puds was always there.

For many years my faithful friend, always by my side,
Alas, I miss every day, from the second that she died.

I kept the photos of her, her toys she played with too,
I loved that dog with all my heart, a faithful friend so true.

Betty Hattersley

The Kaleidoscope Cat

Kaleidoscope sees ghosts by night
Fluffs tail like bottle brush
She wails a feline opera
When all the world's in hush.

A tortoiseshell of multi-hues
Of camouflage supreme
She melts into garden jungle
Ephemeral as a dream.

One moment wicked predator
And next your guileless pet
But within her dwells the huntress
Who has not woken yet.

Paws velvet-soft yet dagger-sheathed
Each whisker, a live sensor
The acme of dichotomy
And cunning fit for Mensa.

Tongue-washed, paw-groomed, fastidious
Diva-Siamese superior
Who sneers at dogs and suchlike pets
As specimens inferior.

You'll fail to beg or bribe her
She eateth as she wishes
A pauper's friend or prince's
On cracked plates or golden dishes.

Yet should I lead a good life
And never do my worst
When my passport's stamped for Heaven, that
Witch's cat'll be there first.

Sarah Blackmore

Dogs

An air of excitement pervaded the hall
Excitement like that at a debutantes' ball,
Dogs all barking, leaping or sleeping,
Flushed female owners emotionally weeping,

Spotted Dalmatians and pugnacious pugs,
Drooling mastiffs with long floppy lugs,
Cheeky York terriers and doleful bassets,
Were all parading their unnatural assets,

They were dogs with long leggy bounds
Like greyhounds and sleek Afghan hounds,
Golden retrievers and glossy red setters,
Refusing to concede they had any betters.

French poodles were there, looking haughty,
Pekinese lapdogs behaving naughtily,
A King Charles spaniel choosily regal
Rebuffing the attentions of an amorous beagle.

Majestic Alsatians and imperial chows
Were dutifully taking their well-earned bows,
Dogs of all shapes, breeds and sizes
Competing for nationally sponsored prizes.

Legions of shampooed and perfumed dogs,
Elegant, pampered and engineered dogs,
Man-made and unnatural, long, short and tall,
But to my mind my mongrel's the best of them all!

F R Smith

Cat Cares

I want a place where I can sleep
And rest my furry head,
Wrap my tail around my paws
In a snug, warm, cosy bed
My needs are few
I don't ask a lot
For my nine lives to be complete,
Love and care and some gentle strokes,
And a few nice things to eat.

Christine Williams

Walking My Dog

Walking my dog
At half-past seven
When it's windy and cold and wet,
Turn up my collar,
Slosh through the puddles,
He's my friend; he's a wonderful pet.

The joggers are out
And other dog walkers,
Traffic is building up fast,
About half an hour
And I will be back
Home, drinking hot tea at last.

Give him his breakfast,
Give him a pat,
Promise him a nice juicy bone,
He looks at me
With big soulful eyes,
Without him I'd be so alone.

June Melbourn

Animals

I'm only a harmless creature
I've got feelings just like you.
So why do they keep me locked up
In a place the call 'the zoo'?

I'd love to have my freedom
To roam over the country wide.
But they've locked up all the gateways
To keep me and my pals inside.

One day the gates may be opened
And we will be free to roam
But we will still be strangers
For we are so far from our home.

D Adams

Mugs At Sixty-Eight

The word spread through the feline world,
'There's mugs at sixty-eight.
You only have to look half-starved;
They'll feed you on a plate.

There's Kattavite and all the brands
Well advertised on telly.
No ginger tom nor Persian pet
Should nurse an empty belly.'

So every mog in Moggyland
Turned up to grab his portion;
Some even seized their chance to make
A bob, by sheer extortion.

You've heard of eighteen forty-nine
When men rushed out for riches.
That's nothing to the scramble that
Ensued in lanes and ditches.

One day a sign was set up, on
A post beside the gate,
The gist of which, translated, meant
'No mugs at sixty-eight'.

As if that wasn't bad enough
For every living mog,
The garden was soon occupied
By an enormous dog.

John Belcher

64

A Dog's Nightmare

Hop, hop, hop, I can see those fleas
Hop, hop, hop, they're going to jump on me.
Hop, hop, hop, here they come across the floor,
Hop, hop, hop, too late, I'm out the door.
If they get in my coat, I'll scratch all night and day,
Then Mother covers me in dust and brushes me that way.
Hop, hop, hop, one's jumped right on my nose,
Hop, hop, hop, another's reached my toes.
Hop, hop, hop, I have nowhere left to run,
Now there's no more hopping, so I guess their job is done.

Mandy Jayne Moon

My New Horse

A new horse, what an exciting day!
A strong piebald lad, gentle eyes and intelligent head -
'A worker and nothing else,' so the trekking centre said.

The week's trial was strange for me;
Just a snaffle bit was all he should wear,
And was told 'He eats nothing more than grass and air
So don't be tempted to feed him lusher fare!'

Two months have gone by, the cheque banked long ago,
But in my mind second thoughts and doubts continue to grow.

He seems to have settled in the field, which is good,
But lost shoes are hard to find and his hooves are so big,
That my budget only allows for refits at a time.

On a hack he wants to go home before we start,
And no amount of cooing can reach his heart.

'A brave soul of sterner stuff I should be!'
But I quail and wish it was some other rather than me!

On the last ride, when my nerves could stand no more,
Little did I know there was a surprise in store.
As I loosened his bridle, he turned his head,
Looked at me with his gentle eye,
And whispered 'Just persist and I'll try!'

Jocqueline Jones

The Calico Cat

The calico cat glides across the cold floor,
headed for the distant door.

Behind the door lies one sick and in pain,
fighting, his strength to regain.

The old cat leaps from floor to bed,
as if being supernaturally led.

The quiet figure stirs,
as the cat softly purrs.

The hand reaches for the cat,
to give him a gentle pat.

The cat remains there throughout the night,
keeping his master in sight.

The day dawns with sun shining bright,
the master stirs at the glistening light.

His strength has been renewed,
and his pain subdued.

As he stroked the cat's head,
he quietly said,

'A creature you are,
but my best friend by far.'

Linda Constantatos

Epitaph

Here lies the body of Halley Hound.
A better dog will ne'er be found.
No more the whimper, wag or woof,
The wet nose on my knee
Nor yet the race across the beach
To plunge into the sea.
She's gone alone, fresh fields to view,
A better dog I never knew.

Maurice Gubbins

Dalmatian

Someone knows the way out of the abyss
Splash, splash, in the bath
A Dalmatian canine habit
Go forward to the next stage

Move it on up
To the top of the class
Where would we be
Without that dog?

Finance ready all the way out
Nobody saving up except the doggy people
Prepaid envelope Dalmatian charities
Passed on to doggy Heaven.

S M Thompson

Cage Covering

Doing budgie-sitting
I had a little chore
Cage-covering it was
But one night I had more
This particular evening
Outward came this sound
'Goodnight my darling'
Stepped back and fell down
Another noise then came out
It sounded just like this
'Please I hope you're not hurt'
Followed by a kiss.

Michael D Bedford

Snowy - Amber's Star

I looked up in the sky last night and saw a twinkling star
It reminded me that though you're gone, you're never very far.
And then the memories started, I recalled them one by one
From the day that I first got you, till your time on Earth was done.
So scruffy and so muddy, to me you were unique
I'd brush you till as white as snow, and trim your little feet.
I'd lead you off and through the gate, in you I had such trust
You'd trundle off into the field, then roll yourself in mud and dust.
Not just my pony, Snowy, my confidante and friend
The one I could share troubles with, your ear you'd always lend.
We had an understanding, you and I, my little lad
You'd always lift my spirits if I were feeling sad.
You'd gaze at me with soulful eyes, I saw devotion there
You'll never know how wonderful it felt to know you cared.
And though the years are passing since the day you went away
I still recall the things we'd done, the good, the bad, the 'so much fun'.
I long for you to be here still, I often shed a tear
Then pain and sorrow grip my heart,
As I remember you're not here
But love like ours is timeless, it cannot fade or die
Always I give thanks for you as I gaze at my 'star' in the sky!

Audrey M Tully

Lament For A Pet Rabbit

The rabbit lopin ower oor green
he wis the finest o them aw,
wi his white jeckit, shinin clean,
an troosers, rabbit grey, but braw.
Oor twa-three cats he didnae heed,
nor yet oor cairnies, wild an yappy.
Aye, he wis brave, but noo he's deid,
       oor puir auld Mappie.

Oor Mappie aye wis clean an neat
but kept his feelins tae himsel.
He'd come when there wis ocht tae eat,
but did he love us? Wha could tell?
Whiles he wad let ye stroke his fur
an gie him lettuce, green an sappy,
but och! A rabbit cannae purr,
       an nor could Mappie.

He wis a rabbit fu o sense
an lovin life, like me an you,
but ae sad day, ayont the fence
we fund him, stiff, an wet wi dew.
But A'll tak Grandfaither's advice
an no be greetin sair for Mappie,
for he's in rabbit paradise,
       an unco happy.

J Waddell

The Escaped Horses

Today I saw a splendid thing:
Five chestnut horses galloping
Abreast in an unbroken line,
Their hooves a-flash, their coats a-shine,
Along the tarmac'd highway flying,
Oblivious of the danger lying
Not far ahead, as cars speed on
Along the Route Napoléon.
No reins nor saddles on them press,
But joyful, free and riderless,
With easy movement fast they go -
Their manes and tails like pennants flow,
Their flanks and limbs awash with light -
Around the bend and out of sight!

Evelyn Westwood

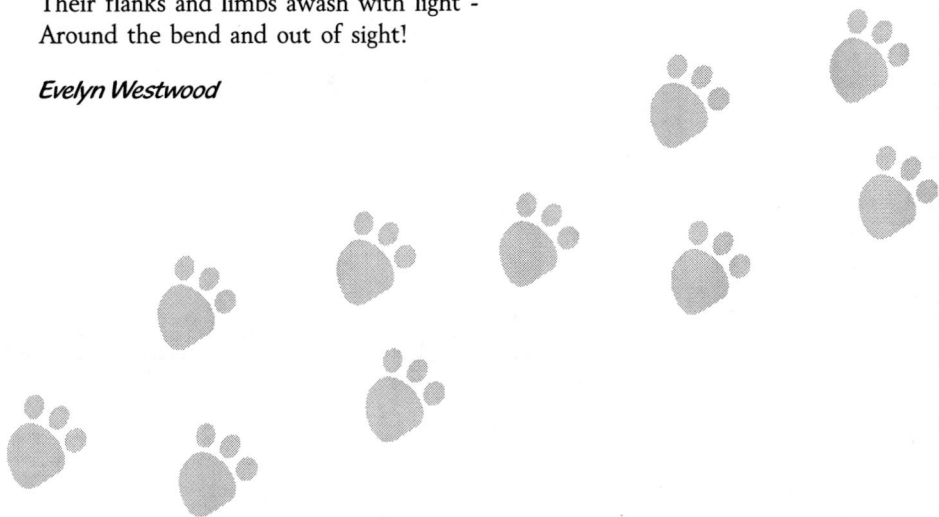

The Guard Dog

'I'll tell you a story,' a friend of ours said,
it made the hair stand upon the back of his head
When he went to an old lady who lives alone,
sadly who is aged and very frail grown

When he found her house, she was waiting for him
beside her stood a large dog, alert, guarding.
Indoors there was no sign of this dog to be seen
as he had died the previous year it would seem.

A photo of this dog was exactly the same
as he saw guarding her and her home down the lane!

Valerie Ovais

A Kitten's Plea

I'm a little kitty
I really need a home
I'm cute, soft and fluffy
And I promise not to roam
I'd be very good for you
And would try hard not to cry
When you're sad and lonely
I'll lick your tears goodbye
We could play with balls of string
I'd make you laugh, you'll see
The fun we'd have together
If only you'd agree
And when my kitten days are gone
And I'm a great big cat
I'll chase the mice when they come in
I'd even face a rat!
So sat yes to this kitty
Go on we'd have such fun
And I will always stay with you
'Cause you will be my mum.

M McNamee

. . . And The Condemned Ate A Last Meal

A flea
With glee
Alighted on my knee.
My cat,
She sat
Close by me and was glad.

Her problem gone,
So she looked on
As I sellotaped the flea
There on my knee

Cat and me,
We are proud, you see
'Cause dead is the flea

But saints alive!
Many more survive
Bent on revenge
My fist I clench,
Then grab the tape.
There's no escape!

To dine on me
Is a death sentence, you see!

Helga Dharmpaul

She

*(Dedicated to Smokie for all her love and affection
which is reciprocated)*

The storm would not let up
Fury would not abate
Hitting me on all sides
Keeping me awake

Trees shook in the moaning wind
Empty milk bottles were scattered
There was no escaping it
Night was turned to day

Finally I had to give in
And go and see what she wanted
Storm in a teacup?
My cat's attitude?
Her Majesty wanted in!

Mary Shovlin

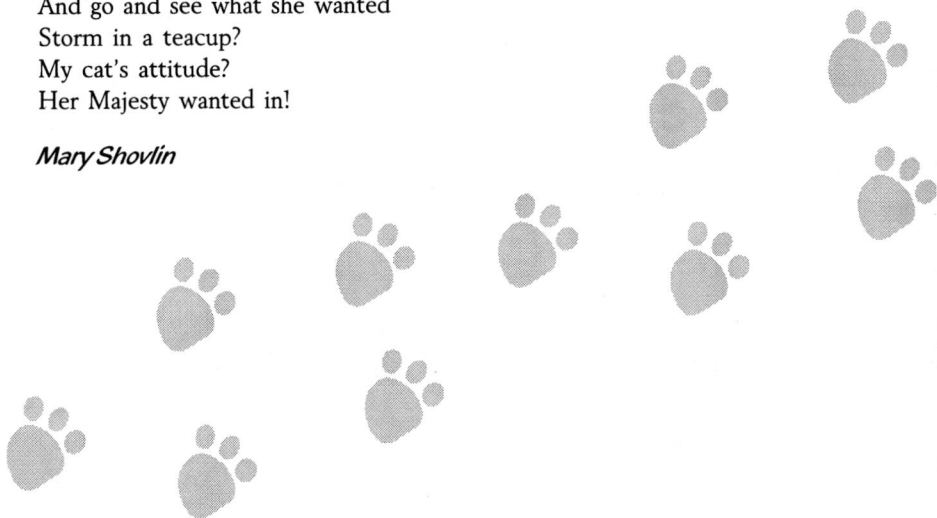

Butterfly

Spread your wings and fly
upwards to the sky
fluttering, rising high
colourful butterfly

A moment you rest
at a flower's breast
clad in your brilliant dress
you receive its caress

On a sunny day
your life is gay
at mere sight
you create delight

Graceful butterfly
continue to fly
enrich nature's globe
with your gorgeous robe.

Wila Yagel

Our Max

(For Melanie)

We have a dog, his name is Max
He is black as the ace of spades
Very fond of chasing cats
He is quite fit for his age.

By trade he is a gun dog
But he hasn't got a clue
He would run a mile if he saw a frog
Believe it or not, it is true!

Jokes apart he is so smart in a funny kind of way
He is faithful and has a big heart
We would not part with him, no way!

May Ward

Jess

Jess, oh Jess,
Good and you're not a mess,
Cos you live outside,
And you're a perfect ride,
Allergic to flies,
But still she tries,
You're my best friend,
I can't imagine the end,
You love your food,
You're always in a good mood,
You are my perfect horse,
Always have been of course,
Your coat so black,
And your elegant tack,
You look like a star,
Even from afar,
Your golden heart means so much to me!
Friends forever, you and me!
                    We're family!

Sarah Herbert (12)

Our Dog

She was an adorable little ball of fluff,
At first she peed on the carpet more than enough,
But this was quickly cured, she learned to do things right,
In the garden first thing in the morning and again, last thing at night,
Then we would go for many walks,
On beaches, fields and often stopping for talks,
With people we would sometimes meet,
Or perhaps whilst resting on a welcome seat.
We loved our dog with all our heart,
We dreaded the day that we should part,
She was good at football and 'pull the rag'
And could have some fun with a blown-up bag.
She could fetch our letters from the door
She gave us her sorrow when our health was poor,
A lot of love and a bit of grub was all she ever desired,
To be at our side constantly was also required,
Her gentle eyes and kindly nature we will never forget,
We cried like babies the night she died,
Heaven now has our dearest pet.

Roy Kimpton

A Dog's Life

My mum and dad are greedy pigs with two legs, not my four,
They never give a titbit, however I implore;
With dark and pleading eyeballs, I gaze from face to face,
For all the good it does me, I'm just a waste of space!

Sometimes when they're cooking, they drop a thing or two
And if I'm quick to lick it, I get to eat it too.
I try to like raw carrot, potato peel and such,
But even on a busy day, they do not drop so much.

But if there's a disaster, perhaps a pot of cream,
I'm right in there with busy tongue, the answer to a dream.
'Good dog,' they say, 'look, here's some more!'
Until I've washed the kitchen floor!

But I stay fit and healthy, wet nose and glossy fur,
While they get fat, just like the cat, except they do not purr.
And there's the real lesson for Dad and for my mum,
Give up all that fancy food and have a tin of Chum!

Patrick Davies

Dog Save Us!

Jim Dog has come to fill my lonely days.
Behold, his head, between front paws he lays,
To watch with soulful eyes unblinking gaze.
With faithful trust he'd gladly die for me,
But he is far from perfect, you may see.

His taste in food to garbage he may turn
And to dig in splendid lawns he'd never spurn.
He loves to bark at non-existent cats
And sprawl on tender plants until they're flat!
When will this dog turn up his nose at smells
As we're on twilight walks upon the fells?

Now you may ask, as you have done before
'So, tell me plain and true, what is a door?'
And Jim will answer you with doggie pride,
'Why it's that thing I'm always on wrong side.'

Gordon Paul Charkin

Barney

I heard the fence rattle and I knew it was you,
As you sprang from the undergrowth into full view.
So confident, so proud, so pleased to see me.
You raced towards the door, tail raised high,
Bursting with happiness - absolute glee.

You followed me everywhere, in the garden and then in the house.
I even remember the day you brought me a mouse!
You played in bags and boxes, sat by my side,
Slept on cushions, chased your dreams, greeted anything new
with eyes so wide.

Such a handsome boy with plush blue and white coat, paws as pink
as a shell,
With a nose to match, beautiful eyes of gooseberry green, you
looked so well.
Everyone loved you; the children would stop at the top of the driveway
And if they saw that you were there, you made their day.

You knew exactly where the sun would warm your fur,
I would watch you gently breathe in and out and when you woke,
that purr,
Sealed your contentment and proved that this was where you
wanted to be.
And so it was, in the summer of ninety-nine, you were given to me -
officially mine!

We shared sun-filled, happy days,
As I carefully watched, learning your ways.
You were my shadow, protecting my land
From other cats, like a sentry on duty, you looked so grand.

Just three years of love and laughter came to an end.
Now my garden is empty - well, not quite,
Seeds brushed from your coat, grow, where you lay.
Forget-me-nots so blue and so bright.

I hope you are playing at Rainbow Bridge, chasing the toys,
I miss you Barney - my beautiful boy!

Theresa M Carrier

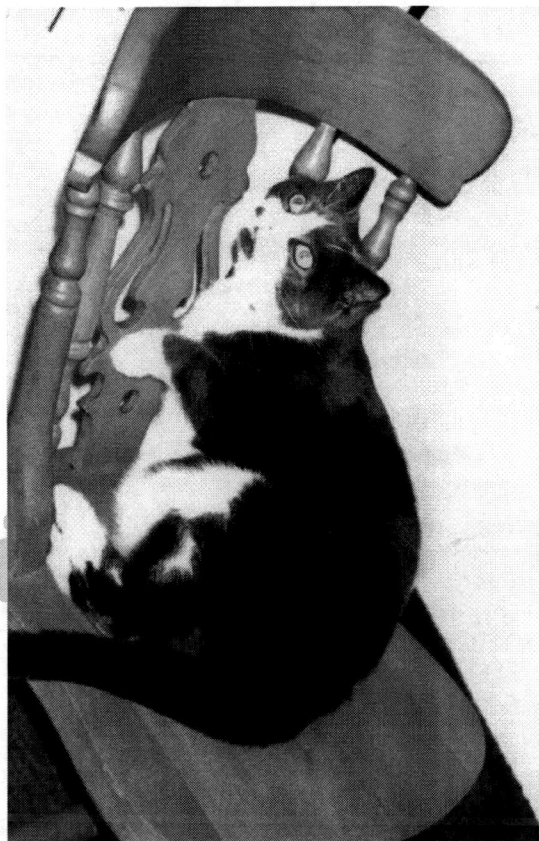

Fred

I shall never forget my favourite pet,
A small Border terrier, Fred.
With a coat full of tufts, he'd have never won Crufts
In spite of his being well bred.
He'd a mind of his own and was famously known
For slipping his lead in a trice,
But he'd always come back at the sniff of a snack,
He was partial to anything nice.
The older he grew, the less he would do,
Growing older is never much bliss,
But if someone had said, 'Will you speak to us Fred?'
Then he might have said something like this:

'Most people attest that I'm long past my best
And well beyond learning new tricks,
That I do very little but salivate spittle
And chase after soggy old sticks,
But a dog of my age is a hard-bitten sage
Who's mastered the art of deceit,
With a sad, doleful look, I can melt any cook
And inveigle a morsel to eat.
When out on a walk, people think I can't talk
Or follow a verbal command,
When they call to me, 'Come!' they imagine I'm dumb
And assume that I don't understand.
But the older I get, the less often I fret,
And, as every old-timer agrees,
It's an old canine trick - to pretend that you're thick,
And it means you can do as you please!'

Alan Millard

86

My New Family

The first time that I saw them I was only four weeks old.
They said that I was lovely and could they take me home.

The second time that I saw them it was plain to see
That they were so excited and they took me home for tea.

I'd left behind my sisters and my mother too;
I was really frightened and not sure what to do.
But I need not have worried, as you can clearly see
I have a new friend, Phoebe, who shares her bed with me.

Louise Holt

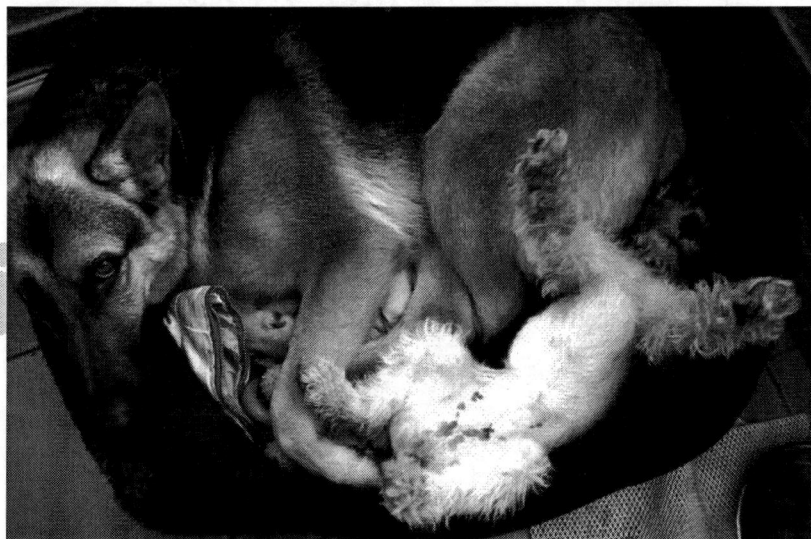

Friends Together

Friends together, poles apart
Hefty, harsh white fur
Experienced wise old mutt
Lumbering, dependable sir

Tiny, dusky damsel
Youthful, frivolous lady
Crazy, risky, comical
She can be really shady

What makes them friends though
Is that they like to chase rabbits
Chase each other
And share each other's bad habits!

Mark Jenkins

Fox Terrier, Sandy Mine

Dressed elegantly, trendy suit azure blue
Ankles trim, black patent shoes
I went for my feathered Vogue chapeau
Left on duvet quilted bed.
Suddenly was overwhelmed in whirling storm
Feathers, feathers white everywhere, nearby, a head.
Hat denuded of feathers, fit to wear no more
Plucked as if for Sunday roast
Duvet ripped open from top to toe!
Culprit, my rascally dog, Sandy
Pedigree fox terrier was he
Instinct, love, hate for fur feathers only
Loyal, loveable friend for twelve years or so.
Creatures, all great and small, kindness give, cruelty abhor.

Ivy Lott

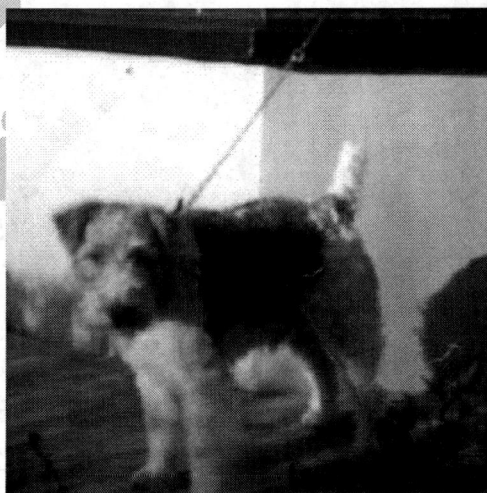

Rudolph

Rudolph is my cockatiel
He's such a lovely bird
He sings, whistles and talks
Like you have never heard
His favourite tune is 'The Cheeky Girls'
He whistles it to his heart's content
He also whistles the sex bomb song
Rudolph was heaven-sent
He's yellow and grey
With big red cheeks
We've had him since
He was just eight weeks
He sits in his cage
Saying 'I'm a cheeky boy'
My grandchildren love him
Better than any toy
He sits on my shoulder
As he is very tame
My granddaughter, Ellisha
She gave him his name
He will be one year old at Xmas
Each day he learns another word
He's wonderful and we love him
Rudolph, our red-cheeked bird!

Heather Dunnfox

Our Furry Friend, Scratch

Well, goodbye old son,
We must have loved you
Because, why do we weep?
Why are we sad and lost
And wonder why you're gone?
No more early calls
No more furry hugs and paws,
Just the memories all around
In the garden, that tiny mound,
You never spoke, but never mind
All those licks were very kind,
These last four years have been
Quite eventful in-between,
Those first scratches at the door
To the peaceful pose upon the floor,
It was a pleasure, you may depend
We're going to miss you, our furry friend.

A Chaldecott

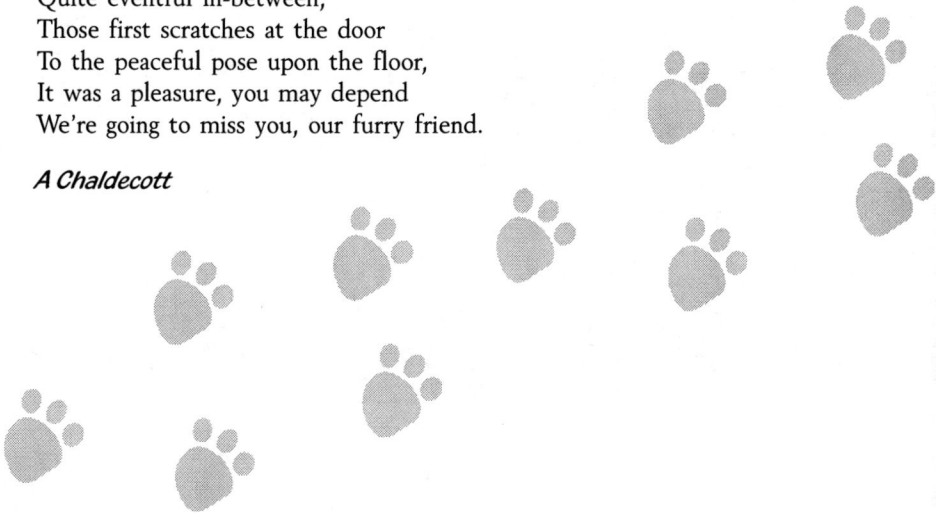

Wedding Fright

I'm getting into such a state
I've been so awfully busy
My wedding's getting out of hand,
It's sent me in a tizzy.

I only wanted one bridesmaid,
That seemed to me enough,
But when my pony friends found out
They went off in a huff.

So now I've said, I'll have the lot
Just to make things right,
But now they argue what to wear,
It's landed in a fight.

Star, she wants a pretty dress
With sprigs of Scottish heather,
But Polly wants a leather skirt
In skin-tight dark brown leather.

Beauty wants a beaded cap
In case there is hot weather,
Honey wants a purple hat,
With a giant ostrich feather.

My brothers aren't much better,
They are a pair of pranksters,
They said they'll only be pageboys
If I let them dress as gangsters.

My intended said, 'You must not fret'
I have the perfect scheme,
We both are going to run away,
And wed at Gretna Green.

Mum, worried by the rising costs,
Said, 'Tell me when and where,
I will drive you to the station,
In fact I'll pay the fare!'

I suppose it's sad it's come to this
I'll not be wed in white,
But a pony in a wedding dress,
Could be a frightening sight.

Sue Walters

Side By Side

She licks him all over, 'til he's quite wet and purrs like mad,
Watching the dog, washing the cat, cheers me up, when I'm sad.
For ages, cat will let dog continue to do its stuff,
But a claw will appear if or when the dog gets too rough.

The neighbours cannot believe how well this twosome gets on,
And dog will bark when she realises her playmate has gone.
They are both young and have several years of play ahead,
Recently, found two fast asleep, side by side, on dog's bed.

S Mullinger

Animals

Toady said to Mole one day
'Let's go into the woods and play
We'll take our food and drinks so neat
And sit and chat and have a treat
We'll ask the rabbits if they would like
To share our humble and appetising fare.'
The field mice are scampering in the sun
'Please come with us and have some fun.'
Otter, Dormouse and Weasel gay
Cry, 'Can we come along and play?'
'Yes, do!' we cry, 'we welcome you
And Freddy Fox, you come too
We'll have lots of games and a scrumptious tea
Then we'll wander homeward full of glee.'

Laura Chaplin

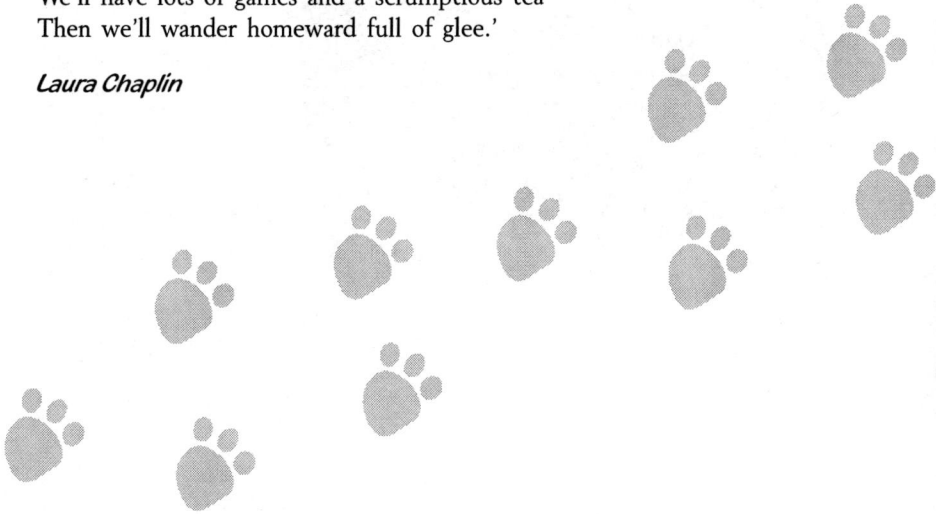

What Is A Moggy?

A bundle of silk purring rhythmically,
Gentle twitching whiskers,
Soft paws draped across a furry chest,
Tail swathed around itself.
A shape of sweet serenity,
It's my feline friend,
Tigger.

S S Marson

Pets

My very first dog was a spaniel called Chum.
An ordinary name for an ordinary pet?
Wrong. For Chum, I'll have you know,
Was by far the cleverest quadruped yet!

Next came Brumas, named for the bear.
A mongrel dog with eyes like dough,
But his tail wagged enough for twenty hounds
As he gambolled madly through grass or snow!

When a guinea pig arrived to take their place
It ate its way through mountains of food,
Then squeaked for more, both loud and clear,
Knowing I'd come as fast as I could!

My final pet, or so I thought,
A master at making one smile,
Suddenly died - as hamsters do -
Leaving us all bereft for a while.

I then decided to try a rabbit,
Called him Alphonse and fed him carrot.
He ran away, which was just as well,
Because I went out and bought a parrot!

Parrots, rabbits, guinea pigs and dogs
We tried them all so what to do?
Take hats and coats, galoshes and gloves
And go see what's to be had at the zoo!

Oriana

Pet

He's only a moggy but he is our pet
We haven't met a better one yet
He's the one we adore
Lying on his back on the floor
Saying, 'Come on Mummy
Please tickle my tummy'
One minute he is climbing all over the room
The next he's playing with the broom
Or racing around the house
Trying to catch that imaginary mouse
Then he is up on your lap
Having his afternoon nap
He has lovely soft paws
Hiding those deadly claws
At night he's out on the prowl
While we wonder what's he going to bring in now?
He likes to lie in the sun to get warm
But soon runs in if there's a storm
He hates to get wet
And yet
He doesn't mind a bath
He is like a rag doll, when he comes out, we have to laugh
We know he's only an old tomcat
But he's our pet and that's that!

Richard Trowbridge

Guess Who?

You're always there to greet me
Whenever I've been out
And if I happen to be late
You never scream or shout
At night you sleep so close to me
You're there when I awake
And while you sleep so softly
There's no sound that you make
I get your meals, look after you
Nurse you when you're sick
It had to be my lucky day
When it was you that I did pick
I can tell you all my secrets
And you never answer back
You mean so very much to me
Even though you're just my cat.

Karen Hodgetts

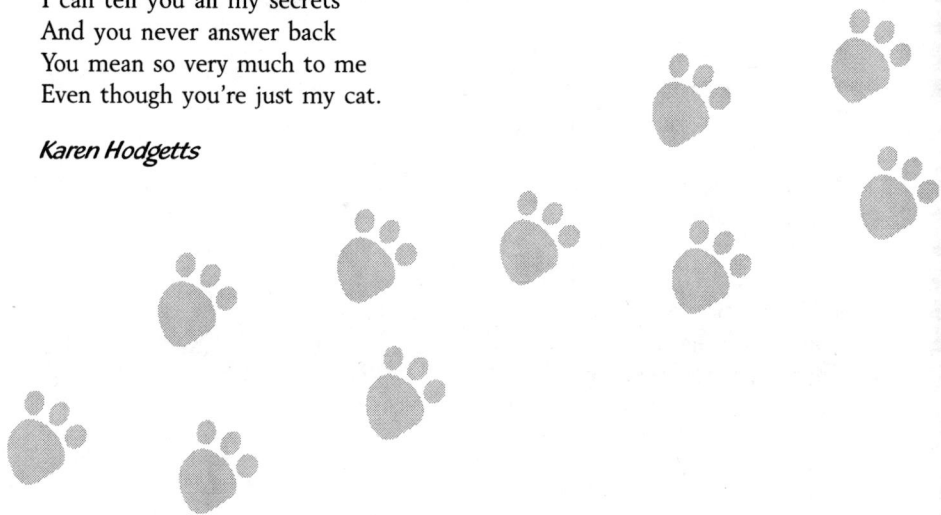

Mitzi - My Cat

Two minutes rest is all I ask
But there's no peace for me.
A little bundle of 'cupboard love'
Is waiting patiently.
My little cat called Mitzi
Seeing that I'm disturbed
Jumps upon my inviting lap
Giving nuzzles and loving purrs.
It's time for food, this cat is saying,
No need for words - just action
And I am so in tune with her
She knows my every reaction
The dish is empty, she goes to the door
And sits there patiently
Why should she use the cat flap
When a doorman is close - that's me?
Two hours have passed, the knocker is raised
I open the door to see
Mitzi is there with a mouse in her mouth
A present for me, you see!
But I am terrified of mice - with a shriek I stand on the chair
Mitzi is startled - so she lets go of the mouse
Who scampers away like a hare.
The chase is on but what can I do?
Thank goodness the door is ajar
The mouse it runs through - the cat follows too
I'm praying the mouse will run far
Mitzi returns like a warrior from war
She looks at me disdainfully
She washes her face - nestles down in her bed
To dream of that present for me.

E Timmins

Polly The Horse

Polly was my grandad's horse,
born after World War I.
She lived a life of cropping grass
with duties almost none;
except for one day in each week
when bridled to the trap
the four of us went for a spin -
denied her pm nap!

She trotted down the country lanes
and made the motors wait
while she took preference over them -
established her estate!
So when she met the crossroads four
with traffic from each side
she boldly stepped across them all
whatever should betide.

But one fine day a policeman came
to do point duty there
and just as Polly reached his pitch
he held his hand in air
to stop the traffic in her line,
then Grandad pulled the rein.
She stopped abrupt with legs apart
to never go again.

The policeman tried and Grandad tried
to coax her on her way,
but she refused to budge an inch
to human's lack-a-day!
Until she'd felt she'd made her stand
to be the top horse in the land.

Owen Edwards

Trouble With Cats

Under the stairs there lived a rat
That no one knew was there.
Except for next door's ginger cat,
Who chased him everywhere.

Well, all this chasing got too much
It really made him blue.
If I could only find old Butch,
He'd tell me what to do.

One fine day he met a mouse,
Who said, 'How do you do?'
They made themselves a cosy house -
In the master's worn-out shoe.

The mouse - he did have sisters,
And very fine were they -
With rather splendid whiskers -
So happily they'd play.

One he was quite fond of
So they courted every day.
'My dear - I think that I'm in love,
Shall we go away?

We'll go and find another house
To start our life anew -
We could bring all the other mice,
There'll be a lot to do.'

Eventually - they found a place
In an attic above some shops -
With skirting boards and lots of space
And no more flipping cats.

Wendy Watkin

102

Silent Friend

She holds a wealth of mystery within her eyes,
Something which us mere humans cannot describe.
I can't explain how those chocolate-brown eyes seep
Into my 'I'm happy, I'm OK' disguise.

How is it that a friend of mine has incomprehensible speech,
Yet she touches my emotions which no one can reach.
I never thought I would find in her a silence, an open door,
A space into which my thoughts should I pour.

I wish others could have respect for creatures of her beauty and grace,
Yet instead superiority belongs to the human race.
Why not appreciate the rich, striking sight,
Of her leaping through the whispering grass, as if in flight?

I thank God for this animal poised before me,
Look at her soft, humble face and I think surely,
Surely this soul there through the pain and strife,
Surely she will be a friend for life?

Elyse Lake

Our God Of Gods

I want you to read my little tale
About our 'Siberian' a silver male
We took him home at six months old
For three hundred pounds he was sold

We named him 'Zeus' it suited well
An indoor cat without a bell
He slept a lot and rarely played
Then we noticed the way he laid

Then after that, we saw him limp
He's not a cat to be a wimp!
So off we went to the vet's that night
They said his knee joints were not quite right

We had some X-rays the following day
They told us the results with some dismay
The knee sockets were too shallow for the balls to remain
Not just in one leg, but both the same!

This is usually found in dogs not cats
His breed is rare so it could be that
He's had this condition from birth it shows
Now what do we do? No one knows

We have a choice of two to make
A major op to undertake
To pin his knees and joints together
Or simply leave him lame forever

The vet says he's not in pain
It's up to us, oh, what a strain!
If he has the op, there are no guarantees
He'll not limp on both his knees.

It will take him months or years to recover
He would have one op and then another
Sleepless nights we've had a few
Wondering what we should do

He's ten months old now and loved a lot
Is he having an operation? No, he's not!
Buying a pedigree kitten, be aware
Read lots of books if your cat is rare?

Don't be put off by what I've said
You cannot foresee what is ahead
He's got some mates now and plays a lot
Two Maine Coon kittens, we have got

His mates are Zara and Zak by name
You can't really tell that he is lame
He's happy and proud, he's our bundle of love
He's Zeus, god of gods, the one above.

Kristian & Victoria Haynes

My Cat

My cat stretches out when she lies on the floor
When I put on my shoes, she waits by the door
She runs after sticks and drinks from the loo
I think that my cat wants to be a dog too!

Elaine Langford

Sheba

She passed away many years from now,
But I still think of her, she was my companion and friend.
She was faithful and loving right up to the end,
I miss her waiting at the gate,
Wagging her tail as I came up the street,
She had that twinkle in an eye, my four-legged friend,
The day she died, my heart was broken,
For I lost my faithful companion and friend,
Though she's gone now, I feel her presence . . .
      my old friend!

S G P Evans

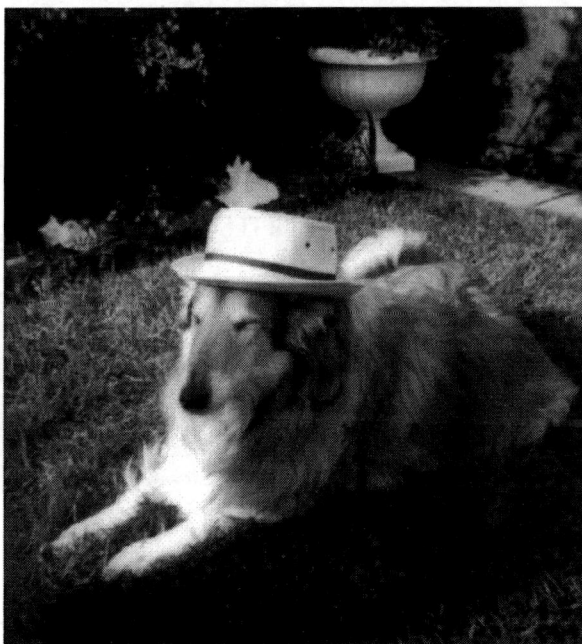

Ike

Ike, our dog, is my best mate
A friend that I appreciate
He's a constant companion by my side
His loyalty and trust he cannot hide

Ike always has a listening ear
No problem too small for him to hear
He's not critical, does not demand
Obeys my voice and any command

He seems to walk with such pride
Head held high by my side
The highlight of his 'doggy day'
Is a walk in the park and then to play

Our cat, Otis, is his best mate
That pair you just can't separate
They whisper secrets in each other's ear
Confident no one will hear

Ike's role in our family
Is an important one as you will see
For we can leave our house at night
Knowing everything's alright

'Cause who is guarding our front door?
Ike, of course, who could ask for more?
So if a pal for life you would like
Choose a dog like my Ike!

Penny Pritchard

Fud

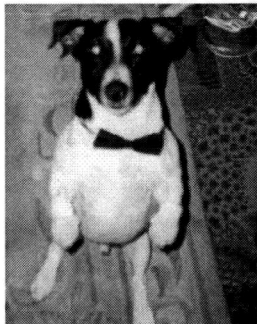

Dear little Fudski pudding and eggs
Has a round fat body and short little legs.
He's a Jack Russell and everyone's friend
As long as you have lots of playtime to spend.
With black circles round both of his eyes
He looks like a badger or even a spy
He has naughty habits, some are quite bad
He steals from his mother, oh what a cad!
Don't leave your teacup on the floor
He will drain every last drop without raising a paw
He plays football with children, bounces balloons off his nose,
Being a Jack Russell, he has the time, I suppose.
He can lie on his back holding a ball in his paws
Turn over and catch it before it reaches the floor
He has a sensitive nature and hates to see you cry
And will jump up on your lap and lick every tear dry.
He will sit up and beg with the patience of a saint,
But don't be fooled, he's not quite that quaint!
He has bad habits, I've not written down
To be honest they are so awful they would make you frown.
The best thing about Fud is at the end of each day,
He will cuddle up close and take all your troubles away.

He thanks you for dinner, walks and, don't laugh!
He will even join you when you're taking a bath!
Dear little Fudski pudding and eggs
With your round fat body and your short little legs
You have your faults, you can be a pain
But whatever your faults, you're loved just the same.

Barbara Archer

My Significant Other

I have a friend so very dear who's like a second skin
He's almost like a shadow, 'cause he's always right behind me.

And when we have our meals, I always share my food
I know I probably shouldn't but it's so hard to deny him!

When I work, he's always there, faithfully watching
Waiting to follow me to see what I'll do next.

Sometimes he'll go to bed and if I'm not ready,
He'll come to gently indicate my company is wanted.

He guards my home so diligently, I shouldn't ever worry
For if evil were a-lurking, he would surely let me know.

He patiently waits for me when I have to shop
And let's me know how glad he is that I've hurried back.

And if I have to leave him which I never like to do,
He is oh, so very sorrowful and does he ever pout!

Impatiently he waits for me and when I return,
His happy shouts let me know how very much I'm loved.

He is very dear to me, this, I hope he knows,
For love is not love, they say, until it is returned.

So why, you ask, don't we wed . . . since our love is so enduring?
Could it be I'm just his mistress, and he is *man's best friend*?

Bonnie Rudzik

Happy Memories

I used to have a dog called Pat
She was so full of fun
Always waiting on the mat
Lying in the morning sun

I miss her every night and day
But the memories are so sweet
She was so good in every way
When curled up on my feet

In the car she loved to ride
To the moors to romp and play
Chasing rabbits in her stride
We all enjoyed a happy day.

Phyllis M Nichols

Monty

I knock at the door
See an innocent paw.
Blue eyes look up at me

And I look at the cat
Sitting on the door mat
Watching with intensity.

It's as if he was waiting,
Like he'd been narrating
A story about me.

Big and fluffy
He's never scruffy
But graceful and sweet

He's as big as a dog
But looks like a mog
And you *have* to give him a treat!

Roisin Fattorini (10)

The Peeper

(From a visitor's perspective!)

I thought I saw
A puddy-cat a cweeping . . .
No - not that!

Not a sliding, rolling thing,
A stretching queen -
It was less serene.

A glimpse -

I think,

Gone in a wink

A twitch

A snatch

Missed with a blink!

Was anything there?

Yes.

Tales of emerald eye and pudgy paw -

Not at all what *I* saw!

Somehow I feel . . . I sort of sense,
That her sighting of me was *more* intense.

Not so quick . . . *not* a mere flick.
But a *lingering* look - could have written a book!

And I absolutely *know*, no doubt in my mind
That her description of me will be *most* unkind!

Regina Fattorini

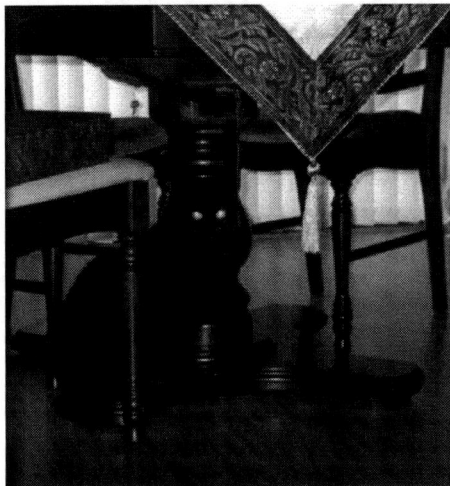

Phoebe

Whenever you want someone to be there,
Not to talk but just to care,
Phoebe comes when you call
And sits by you so loyal and small.

Yes, she snores and has a doggy smell,
But we all love her, so what the hell!
With her toys, Badgey, Hedgey, Furby too,
She'll fetch them and bring 'em to you!

She licks her chops and scrounges so,
That silly old dog, oh she knows . . .
Words like 'garden', 'birds' and 'cat',
She sits 'on guard' from her mat!

Jackie Heath (15)

Rodney And Fudge

Rodney and Fudge are the funniest pair,
They shuffle around without a care.
Their noses twitch in an amusing way,
As they eat our lawn at the end of the day.

Their eyes they stare inquisitively,
As they skip along quite positively.
But I know too well what they search for,
The barbecue they hide under on the floor.

I try to keep them away from there,
And chuckle too at their floppy hair,
Yes, to keep them away, I try my best,
But they get past, my dear little pests!

G White (14)

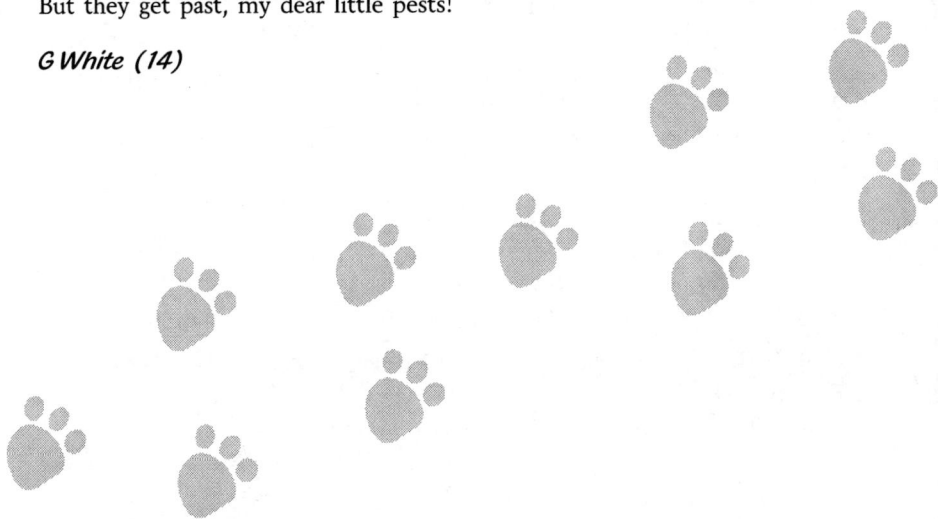

Sophie And Candy, Friends Of The Canine Kind

(or, You're never alone with a Dachshund)

This story that I write is of Dachshunds brave and true,
I'm honoured that I share my home with not just one, but two!
My friends and my companions, who never leave my side,
Sophie and Candy, my little ones, in whom I take such pride.

Sophie, with the long red fur, who walks with regal grace,
A princess among sausage dogs, with a noble intelligent face.
Who sits up at the thought of food, with a back that's ramrod straight,
I know she really wants to clear the dinner from my plate.

She seems to know the words I speak, whene'er to her I talk,
She knows just where her lead is kept, when I say the one word 'walk'.
Ferocious with all other dogs, except for little Candy,
If anything attacks me it's sure good to have her handy.

And what of Candy, small and smooth, with coat of shining black!
What would she say to me, her friend, if she could talk back?
Her favourite word is 'biscuit', she's never far away,
Puppy-like, mischievous, always wants to play.

She rolls upon my towel, when bathing I complete,
Swathes herself with my body's scent then trots up to lick my feet.
These two happy little dogs are not just pets to me,
They're faithful, loyal and loving, part of the family.

Their body language tells me almost all I need to know,
They tell me when they're hungry, or when they need to 'go'.
I know just when they need a stroke, or just a little pat,
You're never alone with a dachshund, my two friends
Make sure of that!

Brian L Porter

Pets

We take our dogs out for a walk
They're pulling all the way
They know where they are going
Because we go there every day
We let them run around the wood
And they just bark with glee
Then he will see a squirrel
And chase it up a tree
But when I whistle and call his name
He comes straight back to me
For her I have to throw a stick
She loves this little game
She's the one called Anne
And Reebok is his name.

C C Lee

Big Fella

Named for a virtuoso
bred from the alley's best
Yahudi
was orphaned young and raised
by a scientist, who loved him like a son.
'Mr Magarian, it's leukaemia
we'll have to put him to sleep'

Big Fella, big mane, big feet
Big Bum is gone,
but not in vain
For 'little fellas' walk the Berkley streets,
tails of a thousand and one heats.

Prince Freakitty Queen Key
And my pumpkin maiden fair
will miss their King Yahudi
who
brought love and respect to the words
'Big Bum'

James Rasmusson

Untitled

Cats can purr
With their glorious fur
They can miaow very loud
Right over the crowd
They chase the rats
And lie on the mats
They sleep all day
And they love it in May
Where they play in the garden
And get out of the way
Cats are sweet
Cats are fine
Think again . . .
Because they're mine!

Melika Gumush (13)

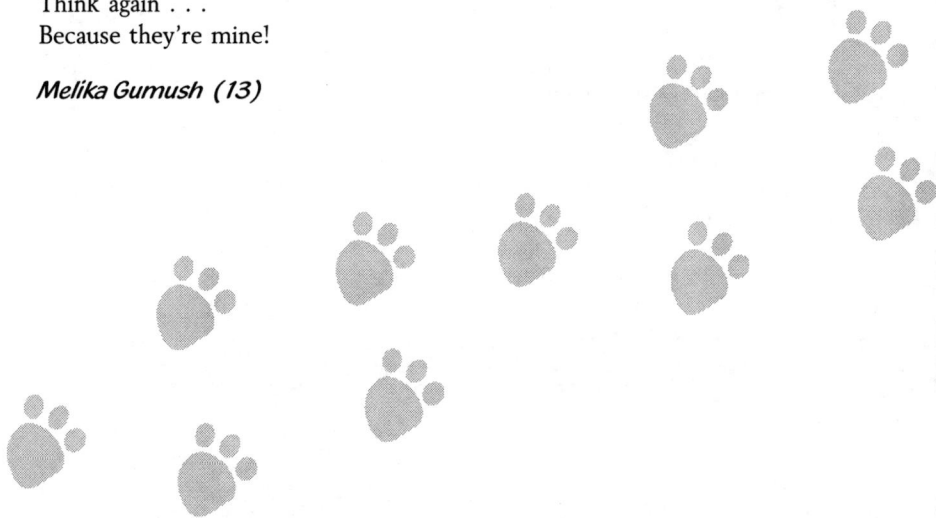

Rentacat

Your silky paws run after me
whenever I appear.
You drape yourself upon my knee
and purr when I am near.
Your liquid eyes compel me
to pause and give you heed.
A stroke upon your glorious fur
is all you seem to need.
A scratch or two behind your ears
to satisfy an itch
and tickling your tummy
can cause your tail to twitch.
Upon the sound of dinner plates
clinking on the side
your weary body stretches up,
your tiny mouth gapes wide
to ask if, just perhaps, there may
be some small titbit there
to satisfy a hungry puss
who only wants to share
each mouthful with his loving friend,
for they'll be buddies to the end.

Well - just until he hears Mum shout,
'Hey, Frankie - come on - dinner's out!'

Helen Strangwige

My Pet Dog, Rufus

Rufus is my puppy
And he's such a playful pet
He loves to hide my slippers
And I've still not found them yet!

He doesn't like tinned dog food
He prefers a juicy steak
And although it's not good for him
His treat is 'Cadbury's Flake'.

He loves me going shopping
Because he knows he'll get a bone
He guards the house and barks like mad
And even answers the phone!

He loves to chase the next door's cat
He has him running scared
My neighbour thinks he's vicious
But her senses are impaired

Because he's such a lovely puppy
He just likes having fun
And although he's only one year old
He's nearly six foot one!

Sandra Booth

An Angel Came Through The Mail

Gizmo, Gizmo, is my one and only.
He picks me up when I'm feeling lonely.
When I'm down or have a frown,
He's always there and comes sniffing around.
He wags his tail, but his eyes look sad,
That stops me from feeling bad.

He's old, arthritic and quite deaf
But he's my life, my soul, my very breath.
God sent Gizmo, he's an angel in disguise,
He came via the mail and saved me from a life of demise.
He's my 'special needs' dog, I love him so much,
His fur is so fluffy, it's a pleasure to touch.
He digs Mom's garden, digs at the moss
He drives her round the bend cos he knows he's the boss!
When he's excited, his eyes open wide,
He's my very own gremlin, but nice inside!

Teresa McTigue

Cats

I love cats
One called Patch
I have owned a few
One called Sue
But is it because I am older
That I am getting colder
Towards the little darlings
One called Marlene
Or is it the piles I find
I can't hide that I do mind
As I have to scrape it up
Such smelly stuff
On top of my plants
The thought of it on my hands
As I pull out the weeds
Before I can sow the seeds
Will they all be scratched out?
The birds are not about
They have been chased off the tree
So I shall not be stroking a cat on my knee
Until they start to cover it up
So that I don't have to scrape it up
Off the plants in my garden
Those darned cats!

Sylvia Shafto

A Cat's Christmas

Christmas is coming
And Binx is getting fat

Zeus is up the tree
Cos he's the Christmas cat

Kiri's singing carols
Spreading Christmas joy

Luna's growling at her stocking
Hoping for a toy

Victor's rolling in the snow
Getting very wet

Marble's wrapping gifts
Just for the vet

Sheba smells the turkey
Wishing for a bite

And Guinness is asleep
Dreaming of a silent night!

Libi Garner

Which Pet For Me

Lost for some company I thought I'd get a pet
So down I went to the local shop to see what I could get.
The man he said, 'A tortoise would be easy just to feed and keep'
But I wanted something wide awake instead of half asleep!

He pointed to some goldfish that were swimming in a bowl
Though they were very pretty, they did not stimulate my soul.
'Perhaps,' he said, 'two long-eared rabbits might be just for you!'
But 'No,' I said, 'it wouldn't be long before I'd have forty-two!'

'So what about a little bird to cheer you when it sings?'
But then I saw the mess it made when it flapped its little wings!
Then I saw a little puppy that I thought I could adore -
Until I thought about the mess he'd make upon the kitchen floor!

I was going to buy a lovely cat who looked so much at ease
But then was told the facts about the worms, the ticks and fleas!
I want a pet that I can keep and talk to when I'm bored
And when I see it every morn can feel my soul has soared!

So I cast my eye all round the place to see what I could see
And it wasn't long before the answer really dawned on me.
It was not a pet I needed, so I've made a cunning plan -
I'm pulling all the stops out - to try to get myself a man!

Cora E Barras

Homer

I have a dog named Homer
Who I rescued from the pound
Nobody knew who owned him
A best friend I really found.

He is a little terrier
Who keeps me on my toes
I lift his lead for walkies
And he dunts me with his nose.

Cold nose and mucked-up paws
Jumping from bed to bed
Shoes all chewed and settee all hairs
He makes me see pure red.

Pulling washing from the line
And ruining all my pegs
Saddened face when I scold him
With his tail between his legs.

I wouldn't change him for the world
He's the best friend I've ever had
So friendly and so loving
I know, I must be mad!

Geraldine McMullan Doherty

Untitled

Soft brown eyes gaze into yours,
A paw gently touches your knee,
He knows you need comfort and that you are sad,
As if into your heart he can see.

How trusting they are, our animal friends,
Never judging or turning away,
They listen to all our stories of woe,
And you know that's as far as they'll stray.

They try so hard to give us support,
And to show that they really do care,
So show them some love and give them a chance,
And your troubles they really will share.

Joyce M Woods

Snake

I had a twenty-foot snake,
It bit me for goodness sake,
I tried to feed it one day,
And it took my finger away.

This got me mad,
Which made it sad,
I fed it mice and boys,
Amongst my play toys.

The police came up to my door,
Said, 'We're taking the thing you adore.'
I had to cry,
As it was going to die.

And now I'm alone,
My life is blown,
My only pet,
Was killed by the vet!

Robbie Strick (13)

Through The Eyes Of Molly (My Puppy)

I wake up with sunshine in my eyes,
I gaze around at the beautiful blue skies.
Contentedly I dawdle over to my water tray,
And take the first refreshing sip of the day.

Out of the corner of my eye, what's this I see?
It's my ball lying in front of me.
I slowly edge towards my prey,
It hasn't seen me yet, it's not moving away.

And in an instant I crouch down and pounce,
I've succeeded in killing it - it didn't move or bounce.
I wag my tail in delight,
And to make sure it's dead, just one more bite!

Uh oh! Now my ball is torn,
Oh well I'm tired, so with a yawn,
I grab my teddy and gently drag it to bed,
And on my warm fluffy blanket I lay my head.

Lianne Bunn

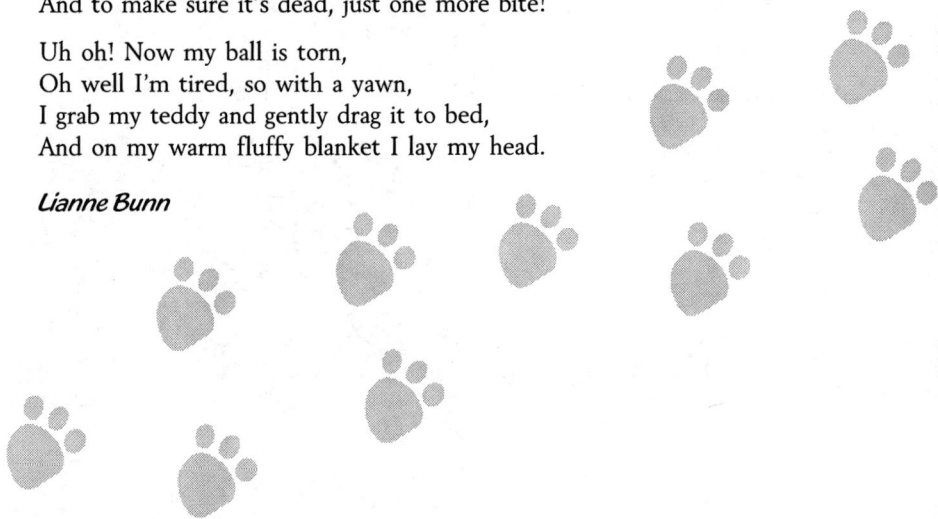

Bunny Em

My Emlyn, long-haired, fluffy, with three black spots on her nose
Is coloured as a Friesian with outrageous podgy toes.
She is my toothless wonder with lop-sided pretty face.
A superstar at ping-pong as she darts about the place.
Em's strange in her affections as she shows her love in bites,
And grapples with me arms or feet, believing it's alright.
Yet who am I to question her expressions of love true?
She is my closest loyal friend, with often-chanted mew.
She likes it when I sing to her, sits staring on the floor,
Then mews in all the places, when I know the words no more.
When finished, then she's purring, one contented happy cat.
I'd never change a part of her, I'm certain sure of that!
Of course there's times she drives me mad, of that I can't deny.
Attention sought, I stop to help, I love her as I sigh.
My Bunny-Em, sweet little Em, you truly are the best,
And on that day when I met you, I knew that I'd been blessed.

Charlotte J Ireson

Oscar's Dream

Stretch, yawn and purr - oh, the place I've just been
Was filled with the sweetest of mice.
They were the juiciest I've ever seen
Yeah - this dream was really quite nice.

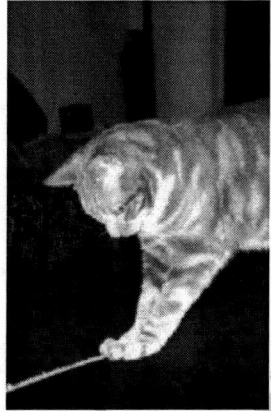

Hmm - what can I do now, where can I stroll?
Sometimes life can be such a bore.
I think I will see what is left in my bowl
And then have a roll on the floor.

I've gulped down my food, now I'll go for a nap
Eating is such a strenuous thing.
Maybe I can find a nice, warm, cosy lap
To curl up and continue my dream.

Ah - there are some legs, all dressed up in black
A lap can't be that far away.
But first these legs could do with a rub of my back
Before I move upwards to stay.

Yeah - now I am pleased, the black's brightened up
With ginger-white clumps of my fur.
His voice shouts, '*Oh no!*' but his hand pats my back
I know he'll be glad when I purr.

Okay, pal, I'm coming - I'm ready to jump
My paws creak - I think I get old!
I land on his knees with a skilled, graceful thump
I'm happy - and *he* won't get cold.

Oh, purr, purr and purr - don't stop stroking my back
It really feels so very nice.
I drift off to dreamland while he scratches my neck
And I'm back with those sweet little mice.

Brigitte Hale

Facets Of A Cat

Crying to go out this sunny morn.
Warmth of amber eyes,
cold at night in stealth and death.

White paleness of the moon,
golden rays of the sun.

Bedecked in black and white,
penguin suit, high on a branch,
watching the world go by.

Tormenting neighbourhood dogs,
chasing neighbourhood cats.

Polite yawn, soft purr, gentle stretch,
licking tongue removes surplus feather,
slinky walk, timeless parade.

Feline majesty, condescending ways
Head of state, head of mine.

Ian W Robinson

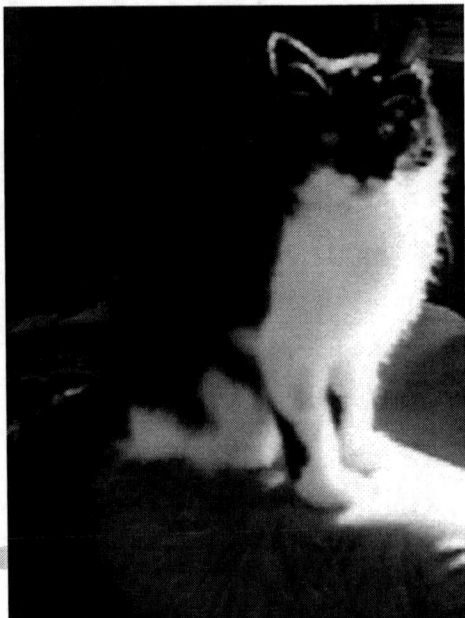

Wild Horses

Wild horses. Free! On the open plain,
Together! No man can ever tame!
Don't harm them, or throw your rope around!
No saddles, no spurs, to slow them down!

Free-flowing their manes of luscious gold
And eyes as black as charcoal
Don't harm them or throw your rope around,
Cruel rustlers! We know you're back in town!

Wild horses don't run from me
They're as free as they will ever be!
They go their way and I'll go mine.
Free till the end of time

So cruel a rustler with a gun
Pulls the trigger and makes the horses run
If wild horses cannot be free
What chance is there for you and me?

What glory to shoot the horses down?
For money? For gold? Or precious stones?
Cruel rustlers, you have had your fun
Come on and lay down your rope and gun!

Pamela Hanover

Birds Of A Feather

The puppies in the window, as usual, caught my eye.
We hadn't got much money and we didn't mean to buy,
But as we went into the shop, just to look around,
We couldn't help but hear this funny little twittering sound.
High up in the corner, in a cage upon a shelf,
Sat two bedraggled budgies, I couldn't help myself -
'Why are those two way up there, sitting on their own?'
'They came to us a week ago, we can't find them a home!'
One was a scruffy yellow, they couldn't tell what age.
The blue one had a broken wing poking through the cage.
'If you take them home with you, there will be no charge.'
So she put them into boxes, and a bag that was too large.
We didn't have the car that day, so we started walking home,
Chatting to them in the bag, pleased I wasn't alone!

The cage we had up in the loft, was once the home of Fred,
The budgie we had till twelve years old, now we had two instead!
The following morning off to the vet, to hear what he had to say.
He didn't think they would live very long, 'but then again they may!'
Their chumminess soon vanished, once we came on the scene.
The blue one, Gill, got jealous and became a little mean.
She knocked poor little Jenny down onto the floor,
But like that trooper that she was, she climbed back up for more!
Back to the vet, he shook his head, her hip was dislocated,
But with a matchstick for a splint, she was reinstated!
Separate cages seemed the answer to this tale of woe,
But the vet then told us, it was time to let her go.
Now left with Gill, she seemed content, to have us to herself.
Anything was better than sitting on that shelf!
But six months on we realised her life we could not save,
We did our best, we think of them and how they were so brave.

Vera Brown

134

Amy

She stares! She stands and stares!
With eyes so big - so green,
A really beautiful little girl,
The prettiest cat you've seen.

And still she stares; and stares,
You look this way and that,
Whatever is she thinking of.
This proud and haughty cat?

But on she stares, just stares,
Then a boyfriend comes to call,
And with a final, distasteful stare,
She disappears over the garden wall.

Avril Hooper

Gemma

I recall the day I brought her home some 15 years ago,
For her master who always had a love of dogs from before,
Yet dreaded having a Staffordshire bull terrier at home.
She was such a pretty bitch, black and white, one just couldn't leave her alone.

She matured and strengthened, always caring and loyal,
And her master was treated like a royal.
After a few years she developed her true form,
That of a magnificent 'Staff' who took the world by storm.

Years of enjoyment, what with puppies and babies around.
Protective and tolerant, she held her ground.
They dressed her up in some ludicrous attire.
At night gentle Gemma was glad to retire.

The solid muscle was erect on her neck
As she galloped up the mountain, a long trek.
The might and power was unique in flight.
One cannot imagine such a magnificent sight.

Then all of a sudden, she slowed down her pace.
Sagging in body, grey hair on her face.
The legs were weary, her breathing not right.
Hearing, non-existent, she was a sad sight!

It's difficult to express in writing, the way I feel today,
Gemma, our old faithful has suddenly passed away.
She was riddled with arthritis and losing weight for a while,
Yet through bleeding and collapsing she didn't die in style.

Today she leaves us with a massive void.
My eyes are so tender, her master so annoyed
As we cannot take in what has happened just yet,
She was part of our family, not only a pet.

Kindness in her face - loyalty as ever,
Can we forget Gemma, our 'Staff' - *never!*

B Thomas

Bath Time

The bath filled, bubbles to the top,
My cat looked on, her next adventure in sight.
She tested the soft foam and purred with delight,
I could see her next move, I tried to halt her delight,
Her thoughts in action, the look on her face.
A soft foam landing in sight!
But the shriek was so loud in cat language
She cried, 'Get me out!'
She was gasping for air, life's just not fair.
Her vice-like grip with no chance of a slip,
The look in her eyes was sheer awful surprise.
I understand what she cried,
'That's just cost me one life, a little too close
To Cat Heaven than I really would have liked!'

Beverley Dales

Walking The Dog

So many different kinds of dogs
Go past my gate each day.
I like to watch their different walks
It's quite a game to play.

Alsatians pad like tigers
With tails held down behind.
There are cheeky ones who mince along
With tails aloft, 'Oh never mind.'

The boxer has a bouncy step
The Labrador, a playful
The Scottie walks with jaunty pride
While some up in their leads get tied.

There are some that have a swagger
With tails to left and right
While some lift legs at lamp posts
And give the cats a fright.

But to everyone who owns them
They're the best dog in the world
With tails up straight or hanging down,
Or simply just tight curled.

Isobel Laffin

Guardian Angel

I kissed you goodbye on a summer's day, when all I could feel was our rain
Knowing I would never have the chance to hold my precious gift in my
        arms again.
I needed to take away your pain, so I placed it inside of me
Without words, you told me, you needed to be set free.
I no longer could watch you hurt, you handed me the lifeline to cut
It was the time for your journey to end, I gave you my heart to take
with you as I lost my fragile friend.
I watched you take the steps to Heaven, your soul fly through the sun
A life together now over, as our new life begun.
I know that peace that only love can bring. I've lost the shelter of my
        angel's wings.
Can you still hear me? Do you feel the sadness my heart now sings?
Sometimes I can hold you in my dreams I wish upon a wish you were still here
Then I feel you watching over me I know now, you're always near.
Your presence graces my earth with all the memories I still hold
Enhancing the miracle of birth in each thought you're there like hidden gold.
I've lost my crutch but I have learned to stand on my own
You're inside me, always beside me, so I can never truly be alone.
I love you,
I will love you until the sun and the moon meet
I will love you until the stars no longer shine
I will love you yesterday, today and tomorrow
I will love you until the end of time.
I know that you are waiting for me at Heaven's gate
For the happiness to return that we had to forsake
For a time we loved and I know we'll still in a million years
And when we meet again in Heaven
My guardian angel can kiss away my tears.

Linda Ann McConnell

140

Three Words

He said the words, 'I love you,' my heart then skipped a dance.
Be joined in holy wedlock, if he got the chance.
These years he is more loving, three words he still does say.
He greets you with a welcome, each and every day.

I look at him in kindness, 'I love you' now he blares.
Poor soul is losing his hearing, no matter, who else cares?
He ages more, yet looks distinct, with a voice all soft and frail.
His 'I love you' is distant as he starts to fade and pale.

I would have been so lonely without this daily rhyme.
To love so deep is natural, it isn't any crime.
I move in close beside him, to repeat that 'I love you'
He's been a friend, a comrade, gave all, that sure is true.

The time has passed so quickly, I wish it could stand still.
His 'I love you' resounded, it gave me such a thrill.
But then one day I found him, all still without a word.
Sadness came across me, at the loss of this old bird.

Teresa Tunaley

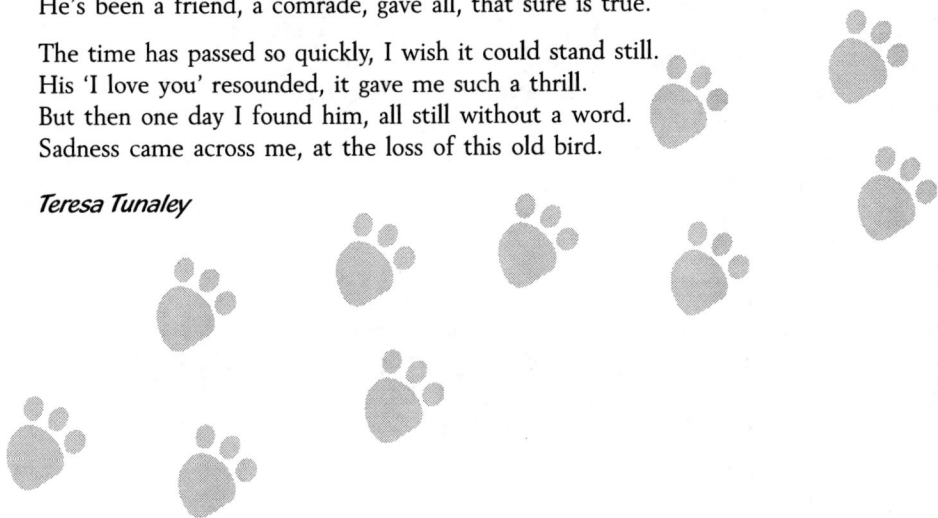

Can't Forget 'Puff'

Can't forget - when I was eight, floodwaters pouring into our garden,
When little brook became a monster river - breaking its banks.
Can't forget - my urgent call to rescue 'Puff' - my white angora rabbit,
And trudging - half-clad - down long path to garden's end -
Where Puff lived in his hutch - hoping he still did!
Can't forget - seeing his little nose - breathing just above water level.
Once - when I tried to pick him up - he badly scratched my arms.
Holding them out to save him now - could Puff see it differently?
I realised then what it means for the Lord Jesus to save me.
But praise the Lord - Puff makes his gallant leap of faith -
Nestles in my armpit - trusting me - I know I must trust Jesus too.
Can't forget I slipped, and could have drowned us both!
Only fence tops visible then - and I was scared to move!
Lord's message to my brain - answers desperate prayer so strangely -
'Success or failure is none of your business now -
Put one foot in front of the other' - so I complied.
While waters still rise alarmingly - it's my time to trust.
Mum receives us home, and warns, 'It's not over yet!'
Towel-dried, Puff retreats under chair by welcome cosy fire.
There - so motionless - we wait - wait - wait - endlessly wait.
O' Jesus, I will wait under the shadow of your wing.

Putting now a plate of carrots and lettuce - tempting Puff to eat
Stranger Lord's message - 'Strawberries'! Why yes, Puff loved those!
Once, he ate all three rows of strawberries from Dad's new plants.
None left! But raid the larder for that strawberry jam -
Separate out its strawberries - will Puff come out now?

Can't forget glorious moment when Puff hops out to eat them,
Lord - I will take care of Puff, I promise, in my love.
You will - won't you Lord - always care for me? O' please, I pray,
Cos Puff and me - we're both saved now!

Don Harris

My Old Pal

Tucked up in a blanket at the base of my bed,
Lies a little old creature who sleeps like the dead.
But every so often with a flick of his tongue,
And a twitch of his paws, he dreams of being young.

'Spirit of Dreams', full of vigour has entered his mind,
Pushed out old age problems and things of that kind,
And now taken over by the joy of this pace,
The years fall away and youth plays on his face.

Welcome back to this comrade that frolics within,
And helps him the battle against boredom to win.
Puppyhood moves in and takes him away,
On a journey of chase, of excitement and play.

There's a little old creature who sleeps like the dead,
Tucked up in a blanket at the base of my bed.
Now, once more exhausted, he'll slumber all day
Ever hopeful that his ally will take him away.

Sara Marlow

Cats And Erm?

Cats are funny creatures when they're first brought to the house.
We show them pretty pictures cute . . . those photos of a mouse.
And say then 'Go and catch one and bring it home to me.'
The cat walks round in circles slow, just thinking hard you see.

Then off it trots its head held high and eyes like laser beams.
It's looking hard at anything that makes a squeak, it seems,
Or has a tail, a pointed nose, or ears like Mickey Mouse.
In every nook and cranny dark, around this big old house.

It's gone just for a whole day now and nowhere to be seen.
Its food untouched, its milk not drunk. I wonder where it's been.
I've looked about the garden slow and even on the wall,
And under stairs, on top of chairs but nothing there at all.

Just then I heard a funny noise behind the old settee.
A sound of rustling paper loud, my cat was there, you see.
But then I laughed till I would burst when looking down at him.
He had the tiny paper mouse . . . that I threw in the bin!

Robert Eric Weedall

Straight From The Horse's Mouth

I'm standing here by the gate,
It's almost feeding time, I can't wait,
If I stand here looking glum,
They'll feel sorry for me then they'll come!
Here I stand with a grumbling tummy,
Waiting patiently for my mummy,
Come on Mum! Where's my food?
If you don't hurry I'll be in a mood!
I'm still standing at the gate,
Please, Mummy, don't be late!
Maybe if I call and jump around?
Hang on a minute! What's that sound?
Clunking buckets! Could it be?
Is she here to feed me?
Here she is, here's my mummy!
With something nice to fill my tummy,
I knew it, I knew it, I knew she'd come!
At times like this I really love my mum!

Julie Roberts

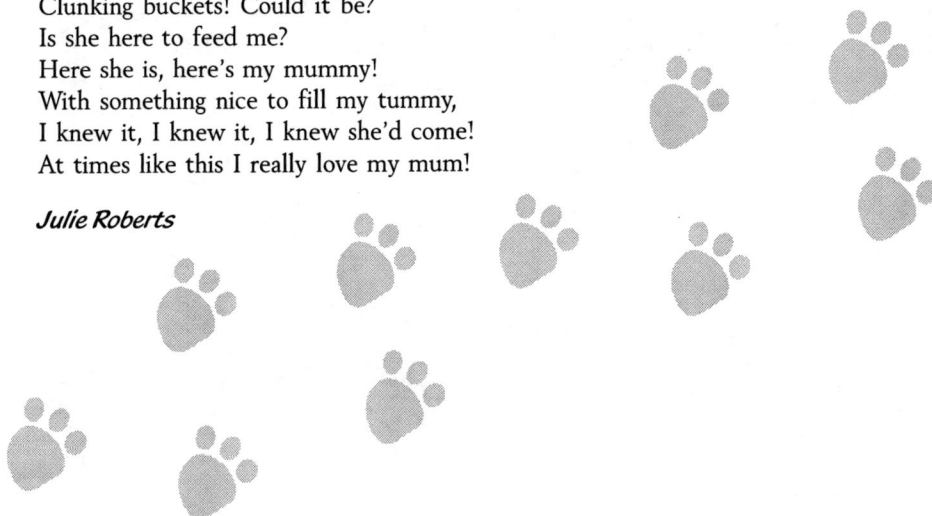

Tibby

I am a cat named Tibby,
My coat is black and white.
When I stick my claws out,
I give my mum a fright.

I like to wash my coat,
And make it gleam so bright.
I also sharpen my claws
And get ready for the fight.

I like to watch the water,
Swirling in the sink.
It gets me all excited
And then I stop to think.

I like a game of ball,
I kick it with my paws,
When you go to grab it
I come out with my claws.

I am such a happy cat,
My people feed me fish
So when I have finished it,
I like to clean my dish.

Linda Finch

Sometimes Her Personality Glows

i watch her
to me it's a bit of a surprise
she is sitting on the back porch
she looks at me with her snowy-glazed eyes
she's getting old now
must be well over ten now
i used to think . . . *she is so old*
but she doesn't look it
sometimes her personality glows

wouldn't say she's a spring chicken
she trips sometimes and walks into the patio doors
but i'd say she makes up for it with her loving face
and her dainty little paws
as a pup she was shown the door
by a cruel owner who would not give her love anymore
she was found and given a loving home
this is her home
she was renamed nala
i used to call her snala
i used to pull faces at her
and tease her quite a lot
she's my sister's family pet
there used to be two
but the angels took the other one
left the family feeling blue
i watch her as she walks in the grass
with her little walk and shaking her little ass
calling after her she's finished her business
runs away she likes no forgiveness
telling her off cos she's ignored me once more
getting frustrated holding onto the door

she walks past me and turns her head as if to say
'ha ha uncle ste, i always get my own way'

i have one thing to do before i go back home
i'm gonna buy her the biggest marrowbone . . .

Stephen A Owen

A Letter From George

Just a little note to say
I have moved away today
My mummy is feeling very sad
But in a while, she won't feel so bad.

For she has found me a nice new home
A place where I will never be alone
I'll be with John and Rosy too
They have told me, 'We love you.'

I know that I'll be happy here
They think I am a little dear
I won't have to stay in my cage
To sit and scream and shout with rage.

I'll be out every day
Lots of room for me to play
It is best for me I know,
My mummy loves me, so she let me go.

Pauline Nind

A Pet

'Mam, you said you would get us a pet
One that doesn't need lots of trips to the vet
A dog or a cat would be lots of fun
But a snake would be difficult to take for a run
So Mam, we'll leave the final choice up to you
But don't get us something that belongs in a zoo.'
'Son, I wouldn't even mind a pig or a steer,
After all I've lived with your father for twenty-odd year!'

Mick Gayfer

Basil Bird

As a child I always wanted a parrot - an African grey,
And teach him lots of funny things to say.
But my parents refused and I had to wait,
Then I had one at last, when I was 28!

Basil's his name and he's a lovely chap
Who flies from his cage and onto my lap.
I'm always amazed at what he can say,
And the swear words he knows, didn't come my way!

He says 'Good morning' as the lights go on,
And cheers me up with his chirpy song.
He listens intently to all noises around,
And can copy exactly - any sound.

The microwave rings and over I go
But is the food ready, almost certainly no!
Basil it was - he mimicked the sound
While the food in the microwave goes round and round.

The telephone rings and he shouts, 'Hello,'
And how many times have I answered the door,
Then realised it was Basil again mimicking the chimes?
He's tricked me with this over a 100 times!

When I sit by his cage, in my comfy armchair
He throws his nuts and seeds into my hair.
He loves being naughty and when I react
On he continues with his cheeky act.

Although he's well fed, 'I'm starving,' he'll say
When we're all having dinner at the end of the day.
He'll squawk and beg until we give in,
There's simply no chance of him being thin!

Enfys Evans

Sweet And Loving Memory

Uncle Fred, he had a budgie
Jo Jo was his name
He talked and learned a lot of tricks
And was so very tame

Uncle was dying of cancer
Spent many hours alone
Jo Jo was his pride and joy
In that quiet little home

Uncle played the saxophone
When he was young and strong
Sometimes he'd have a practice
And Jo Jo landed on

The buttons and the sound-piece
He did not mind the noise
Up and down the instrument
Sideways, and with such poise

When Uncle felt quite tired
And lay upon his bed
Jo Jo, too, went with him
And nestled on his head

When Uncle was sadly taken away
Jo Jo stayed locked inside his cage
He missed his loving master
His sadness unassuaged

He pined and pined
And soon his life had gone
His soul, gone to find his master
In that grassy, peaceful home

Those bright green feathers nestling
On the dark and curly head
A picture I will never forget
When I think of dear Uncle Fred.

J Howling Smith

Dogs

Dogs, dogs, dogs,
from the littlest corgi to the greatest Dane,
fluffy dogs, hairy dogs, tiny dogs, smelly dogs,
all kinds of dogs from all kinds of places,
naughty dogs roll in smelly things,
dig up holes,
chase moles,
clever dogs fetch sticks,
learn to do all kinds of tricks.
My dog's naughty, he doesn't do what he's told,
but even though he's a pest
he's still the very best!

Katie Ireson

My Proxy Pet

To our neighbour's home he came
A small bundle of delight,
Arriving safely on Christmas night

Unable to afford my own
I pretend the doggie's mine
And we both have a good time!

No poop to scoop,
No bills to pay
Rolly and I just play all day!

Helena Henning

Matthew, A Little Rascal Of A Rabbit!

At first, he seems quite the little innocent,
But if only you knew how many females he had made pregnant!
It's utterly disgraceful although that's his job,
And that's why he's not for sale.
You wouldn't be able to trust him!

And if he's bored from running in circles around his pen,
He lets you know fairly fast.
He'd terrify the life out of anyone who has never been in
the store before,
Because as you're walking down the aisle, something on top of the
pen catches your eye.

When you look directly at it, it appears as though there's a rabbit
Propped with his front paws hanging over the side
And his ears flopping down onto his back.
You blink and look again, but the rabbit is gone.
If that happened to me, I'd think I was going mad,
But the rabbit really was there.

He sits down and you think he is going to sleep,
But he gathers all his strength and suddenly springs into the air.
He goes up vertically and on the way down,
He grips onto the corner of the pen tightly.
There's a strip of metal running around the inside of the pen,
And he sits on it, looking quaint and comfortable.
He tries to get over but his rear is too awkward
And he usually loses his balance, resulting in falling.

He lands on his feet and glances round suspiciously,
To make sure that nobody noticed the humiliating fall,
And once he's satisfied that no one saw him,
He settles down for a nap.

Moya Muldowney (15)

ANCHOR BOOKS
SUBMISSIONS INVITED

SOMETHING FOR EVERYONE

ANCHOR BOOKS GEN - Any subject,
light-hearted clean fun, nothing unprintable please.

THE OPPOSITE SEX - Have your say on the opposite gender.
Do they drive you mad or can we co-exist in harmony?

THE NATURAL WORLD - Are we destroying the world around
us? What should we do to preserve the beauty and the future of
our planet - you decide!

All poems no longer than 30 lines.
Always welcome! No fee!
Plus cash prizes to be won!

Mark your envelope (eg *The Natural World*) and send to:
Anchor Books
Remus House, Coltsfoot Drive
Peterborough, PE2 9JX

OVER £10,000 IN POETRY PRIZES
TO BE WON!

Send an SAE for details on our latest competition!